Carol

Love is
Never
Wrong

Warm

Regards,

10
smart
things
gay
men
can
do
to
improve
their
lives

10
smart
things
gay
men
can
do
to
improve
their
lives

joe
kort

alyson books
los angeles

NOTICE TO READERS

MANUFACTURED IN THE UNITED STATES OF AMERICA.

THIS TRADE PAPERBACK ORIGINAL IS PUBLISHED BY ALYSON PUBLICATIONS,

P.O. BOX 4371, LOS ANGELES, CALIFORNIA 90078-4371.

DISTRIBUTION IN THE UNITED KINGDOM BY TURNAROUND PUBLISHER SERVICES LTD.,

UNIT 3, OLYMPIA TRADING ESTATE, COBURG ROAD, WOOD GREEN,

LONDON N22 6TZ ENGLAND.

FIRST EDITION: AUGUST 2003

03 04 05 06 07 **a** 10 9 8 7 6 5 4 3 2 1

ISBN 1-55583-782-4

LIBRARY OF CONGRESS CATALOGING-IN-PUBLICATION DATA
KORT, JOE.
    10 SMART THINGS GAY MEN CAN DO TO IMPROVE THEIR LIVES / JOE KORT.—1ST ED.
    INCLUDES BIBLIOGRAPHICAL REFERENCES.
    ISBN 1-55583-782-4
    1. GAY MEN—PSYCHOLOGY. 2. GAY MEN—LIFE SKILLS GUIDES. 3. GAY MEN—CONDUCT
OF LIFE. I. TITLE.
HQ76.K67 2003
305.38'9664—DC21   2003049779

CREDITS

• "EVERYTHING POSSIBLE" © 1983 BY FRED SMALL. USED BY PERMISSION. ALL RIGHTS RESERVED.

• COVER PHOTOGRAPHY BY GLENN TRIEST.

• COVER DESIGN BY MATT SAMS.

Contents

Introduction
What Works? And What Doesn't?

Alan was a 34-year-old consultant for one of the car companies in Detroit. He came to see me after experiencing depression over his gayness and his relationship with his partner of five years. He'd been seeing a heterosexual male therapist in town but felt he wasn't getting anywhere—either with accepting his homosexuality or resolving the conflicts in his relationship. His therapist referred him to me, telling him that I was gay as well.

Alan was handsome, with boyish looks and tightly cropped hair. His body testified that he was involved with sports—he played soccer and baseball on a regular basis. For his first session, he came to my office dressed in his work attire—tie, white shirt, and wing tip shoes.

"Look at me!" he said. "I don't look gay. You don't either. Maybe we're fooling ourselves. This is just wrong! This isn't how I envisioned my life. I wanted to be straight, with a wife and kids by now!"

Alan filled me in. Six years before, he had been engaged to a woman—then broke up with her. Secretly, he'd promised himself that if their relationship didn't work out, he'd act on his gay feelings and come out of the closet. He didn't want to make any other woman suffer with his inability to commit to her. He knew why he could not commit—he was gay. He could have sex with women, but found it unfulfilling.

On the other hand, Alan didn't like being gay. He felt he was giving into urges he was supposed to repress. He was horrified at the idea of being out and open with others—particularly his family—knowing he was gay.

Alan came from a rural town in Michigan, where his family still lived in the house he grew up in. Nothing had been painted. The furniture never changed. Appliances from his childhood, aside from ones that absolutely had to be replaced, were still there. It was as if time stood still. His parents had stagnated, plugging away in the same jobs they'd had their whole adult lives and drinking at a local pub they frequented every weekend. On a few occasions when he was a child, Alan recalled, his parents took him along and left him and his siblings in the smoky pinball game room while they went to drink in the bar.

Alan couldn't conceive of admitting to his parents that he was gay. "That will never happen," he told me. "They would die! I can't do this to them."

Soon after Alan came out at a local gay bar he met his partner, Matthew. Alan had done little or no dating before Matthew. Being with Matthew was fun and exciting at first, but after the second year Alan felt unhappy because their relationship was in a rut. Alan wanted to integrate his life more closely with Matthew's—he wanted the two of them to live together.

Matthew initially agreed to their living together, but whenever it came time for either of them to move in with the other, or to sell both houses and buy a new home together, Matthew came up with some reason why it wouldn't work out. This conflict simmered for three years.

In addition, Alan was angry at Matthew for not wanting to spend more time together. They saw each other once during the week and once over the weekend. Matthew claimed that with Alan in his bed, he couldn't get a good night's sleep and couldn't function well at work. When Matthew resisted making any move or changing his behavior, Alan would lash out. They would argue, and Alan would become enraged, shout, and slam doors.

Alan admitted that part of the problem was his worry about what other people might think if they knew he was gay. If he went out to dinner, he didn't feel people were staring if he went with a male cowork-er, but he admitted feeling that if he and Matthew went to dinner, everyone would know they were gay—much to his embarrassment.

Though Alan complained about Matthew's avoidance, he was stuck in a pattern of unhelpful behavior too—with a large amount of internalized homophobia about being gay. He blamed his diffi-culties on the closet and on living in Michigan, and he resented Matthew for not participating more actively in their relationship.

In our work together, I tried to help Alan focus on his childhood, because he seemed to be replaying exactly what had happened to him then, back when his parents neglected him. Now he found himself with a partner who, he felt, also neglected him. His frustration with Matthew was understandable, but his high level of anger was an overreaction. It belonged to his parents.

He said that my making the connection to his childhood made logical sense, but he wasn't experiencing any angry or hurt emotions toward his parents. "They did the best they could, and it makes me feel bad to think they did anything negative."

No matter how much work Alan did, in both individual and group therapy, he couldn't reach his true feelings about his parents. He came to my workshops for helping gay men heal and rid them-selves of self-hatred and homophobia, went to gay events around the community—and still felt bad about being gay. He stayed closeted at work and to other members of his sporting teams. His relation-ship with Matthew stayed the same, even though many times Alan threatened to end it.

Finally, though, it was Matthew who broke it off. One night at Matthew's house, Alan became so angry he threw something across the room and broke a window. Matthew told him he'd had enough and ended the relationship.

Now Alan found himself in a bind. Not seeing any progress, he'd dropped out of the gay men's group the year before, and he had no network to support him. His symptoms of depression grew worse. He couldn't tell his family what was going on, and he had no one else to talk to but me.

Isolated and alone, Alan was back where he was as a child, but he continued to deny that his childhood was at all related to his current situation or that his overreaction to Matthew's distancing relationship was really a replay of how he'd felt as a child.

I didn't think Alan could make much progress until he decided to live more openly, and I told him so. I felt that he'd find, stored away in his closet, many other feelings and memories about his childhood. But he wasn't ready to deal with it all. I expressed concern that he'd keep feeling isolated, lonely, and abandoned—unless he addressed the issues of his parents' neglect when he was a child.

Many of us find ourselves in a place like this. I'm a psychotherapist who specializes in Gay and Lesbian Affirmative Psychotherapy and Imago Relationship Therapy, which is a specialized program in helping people with relationship issues, men's issues, childhood sexual abuse, and sexual addiction/compulsion. Over the past 18 years, I've treated literally thousands of gay men in the Detroit area—in one-on-one individual therapy, ongoing group therapy, in workshops for singles, and for partnered couples.

Again and again, I see clients make the same mistakes. And inevitably, I find myself giving dozens of clients the exact same advice.

Reading this book, I hope you'll recognize the stumbling blocks, both internal and external, that have held you back from living an effective, totally fulfilled gay life. Each of these 10 smart things is an antidote to a specific problem that clients have brought to my office time and again.

Through my work with clients over the years, I've seen what works and what doesn't work. Now I'd like to make these "prescriptions" available, in book form, for every gay man to use.

These 10 smart things constitute a kind of checklist—answers to the challenges any gay man may face, at one time or another, throughout his life. Yes, *every* gay man can score 10 out of 10 if he wants to. But none of these chapters is a cookie-cutter, one-size-fits-all prescription. Throughout, I'll give you real-life examples based on my work with clients who put these basic principles to work in their own way—almost always with considerable success and satisfaction.

I ask every one of my clients (and everyone who reads this book) to recognize that he's a unique individual. Health and happiness are your birthrights. And yes, you happen to be gay. So to live a rewarding life as a gay man, you must tailor anybody's advice—mine included—to fit your own particular goals and circumstances, always keeping your own values, lifestyle, and personal strengths in mind.

In upcoming chapters, I'll introduce you to gay men who've crippled themselves emotionally (and often sabotaged their romantic relationships as well) by not coming out to anyone except themselves, their partners, and a few close friends. In most cases, their self-protective impulse only serves to keep them isolated. You'll also meet heterosexually married men who in their 40s and 50s came out of denial and admitted they were gay all along. They experience a profound sense of liberation when they find the courage to come out, being honest with themselves and their families.

You'll read how coming out to your family can reawaken—even worsen—the dysfunctional problems that have laid dormant in the closet. But you'll also learn how men from 15 to 57 have forged deeper, warmer bonds with their parents, siblings, former in-laws, and, in some cases, their children.

I'll explain why gay men are so often criticized for being "childish" or "immature," and how to avoid succumbing to gay culture's overemphasis on looks, youth, and glamour. Afraid of growing old? I'll offer you numerous remedies, including meaningful involvement in your local gay community serving as a mentor and giving other gay men (both younger and older) the benefits of your own hard-won experience.

I will explore with you the specific ways that sexual addiction manifests in the gay male community. Most cases of sexual addiction are rooted in childhood sexual abuse and often respond to a combination of individual and group therapy. You'll learn why so-called reparative therapies—to "cure" our homosexuality—can't possibly work. At the same time, you'll learn about the genuinely helpful "therapy workout" opportunities available to every gay man. Is the best therapist for you male or female, gay or straight? Stay tuned!

Perhaps most important, I'll show you how to keep your romantic relationship with another man alive and evolving as you both pass beyond the first stages of infatuation, through the inevitable power struggle, and on to deep and abiding love.

Believe it or not, your most serious quarrels and disagreements are potentially healthy and can lead to tremendous personal growth for you both, as partners and as individuals.

Even if a wedding or commitment ceremony doesn't feel appropriate for the two of you, you'll want to read about other gay couples who have taken that courageous step—with all the frustrations, surprises, and joys that went with it.

You don't need to be a Mensa member to do smart things and to start reaping the benefits. Hundreds of my clients have already proven to my satisfaction (and, more important, to their own) that these choices *work*.

Psychology can seem dauntingly complex, and sometimes a bit scary. Might there be some things lurking down in your subconscious you'd rather not hear about? No need for timidity. I will work to keep things as clear, accessible, and practical as I can. My clients—from their early teens to their 70s, from every walk of life—help dramatize the issues and hassles that every gay man must face. Armed with their wisdom, clarity, and understanding, you can make personal breakthroughs while still enjoying the special advantages that gay culture has to offer.

You need not agree with every word I say. While reading about the dozens of gay men who came to me for help, however, you're sure to recognize many of the challenges you're facing right now.

Every one of these 10 smart things has the same goal: to help you live *happily*, *confidently*, and *successfully* as a gay man—inside and outside the gay community.

Chapter 1
Take Responsibility for Your Own Life

IT IS HARD TO LOVE YOURSELF MORE THAN
YOU HAVE BEEN LOVED.
—Charlotte Davis Kasl, Ph.D.,
author of *Finding Joy: 101 Ways to Free Your Spirit*

True: It's hard to love yourself more than you have been loved. But while it is difficult, it's not impossible! Let's see how you can love and empower yourself as a gay man.

Many gay men who walk into my office know that I specialize in both sexual addiction and sexual compulsion. They may sound the same, but in fact they're quite different. Patrick Carnes, who coined the term *sexual addiction* in 1983, views the problem as an addiction, best treated by 12 Step and behavioral approaches. Eli Coleman, an award-winning sexologist and author of numerous books and articles on sexual compulsion, feels it's a compulsive sexual behavior defined by anxiety-reduction mechanisms rather than by sexual desire. In other words, he believes that the sexual behaviors are a means of reducing the levels of anxiety the person suffers from and not about a high sexual desire or addiction. And still others believe sexual compulsion is a repetition disorder, best treated by understanding whatever underlying conflict is being acted out. (For a full explanation, see Chapter 7.)

Nick and his partner, Rolf, had been together for five years and had just relocated from California. They came to see me because one year earlier, Nick had logged onto their shared computer and found E-mails from other men, some with nude pictures attached. When confronted, Rolf admitted he had a sexual acting-out problem. He confessed that up to that point in their relationship, he'd had sex with many other men. Ever since, the two had struggled to get back to a safe, trusting relationship.

Rolf claimed that since his original confession he'd had sex with no one but Nick. He was adamant: "I've done nothing!" But Nick was still distrustful and didn't believe him.

During the six months they came to see me, Nick stated that Rolf's behavior only reinforced what he already believed about the gay community: Monogamy is a joke and a myth! All gay men are promiscuous and have lousy moral values. Nick was angry and disappointed that "gay life has to be this way." He remained with Rolf only because, as he confessed, "I don't believe it's any better out there with those guys who parade in drag or in leather and give gay men a bad name."

Nick simply wanted Rolf "fixed." He wasn't willing to look at his own role in their relationship problem. Dutifully, Rolf started to attend my sexual addiction therapy group, as well as Sexual Compulsives Anonymous, a variation of Sex Addicts Anonymous for gay men. (For more information on various 12 Step groups available, see Chapter 5.)

In our work, I pointed out that sexual addiction and promiscuity aren't unique to the gay male community. All men face these issues. Scan the tabloid headlines at the supermarket checkout and you'll see that cheating and promiscuity are challenges for straight people too. Nick had bought the common stereotype that many ignorant people preach: that we gay men are sexual beings only, nothing more. (Behavior that we might call promiscuity is sometimes really a symptom of postponed adolescence. More about that in Chapter 4.)

Very often, sexual addiction results from sexual abuse in early childhood. There's help for these people, and Rolf was getting it. But Nick wasn't willing to explore how his own past contributed to their relationship. In fact, his own childhood was traumatic. His parents had abandoned him, leaving him to be raised by an aunt and uncle, separated from his siblings. Despite this obvious source of suffering, Nick felt that Rolf's behavior was all they needed to address.

Even though Nick denied it, I suspected that it wasn't really Rolf but his own parents whom Nick wanted to condemn for not staying committed and being there for him. In Chapter 9, I explore why we choose partners who remind us of familiar, beloved caretakers from our childhood—and what happens as a result. In this instance, Nick was projecting—transferring onto Rolf his negative feelings and beliefs about his family and gay life in general.

In the end, Rolf continued to work on his own issues, but Nick left him, without ever resolving their situation. Predictably, Nick met other partners who fit into his assumption that gay men couldn't be monogamous and committed to him. Because of his unwillingness to look at himself and to resolve his own personal issues, he never learned different.

An ancient Chinese proverb states that a long journey starts with a single step. The point, of course, is that determination is the key to any endeavor. Without that do-it-yourself resolve to *make* things happen (as opposed to *waiting around* for them to happen), any attempt at a successful life—gay or otherwise—is doomed from the get-go.

Very often, my clients begin conversation by talking about how society marginalizes us gay men and forces us into being sex junkies. They complain that they can't do anything about it because gay male culture supports sexual addiction. I remind them that heterosexists and homophobes do marginalize us. And yes, there's a strong emphasis on sex in our community. But that doesn't mean we have to live that way. (In Chapter 5, you'll discover how to ward off sexual addiction.)

Gay men entering my office also know that I'm a certified Imago Relationship Therapist. Often, like Nick, they want me to help them figure out what's wrong with their partners, who need to change.

Instead, we talk about what their partners might say about *them* and the troubles that their partners might be having with *them*. When each partner takes responsibility and vows not to point his finger at the other, only then can we begin to examine what contributes to problems in the relationship,

Trying to fix another person is a dead-end road. More important—and far more effective—is to make the effort to clean up your side of the curb. Once clients are able to do that, they can realistically examine whether their relationships can survive. Luckily (as you'll see in Chapter 9), they often can.

The 12 Step Serenity Prayer goes: "Grant me the serenity to accept the things I cannot change, the courage to change the things I can, and the wisdom to know the difference." Over the years, some people have modified it as follows: "Grant me the serenity to accept the people I cannot change, the courage to change the only person I can change, and the wisdom to know who that person is—me!"

In my practice, I see a lot of gay men who don't get this. Until they recognize who that person is, true change remains beyond their reach.

Other clients complain that the gay community (particularly Detroit's) is "superficial," "cliquey," "picky," or "judgmental." After further conversation, it's apparent they're voicing more of their own internalized homophobia. In the next chapter, you'll meet one of them, Carl. Once Carl identified the negative lens he used to see the world, his issues with our gay community were greatly reduced. Feeling better about being gay, he started to let go of many of the judgments he'd held about other gay men. He realized they simply reflected how he felt—or more exactly, how he had been taught to feel—about gay men.

Yes, some of the judgments of men like Carl are based on reality. But learning how to create your own reality is the real challenge.

Other men begin our conversation by trying to explain why they didn't come out earlier in life. They hold society responsible: "That was the 1950s [or the '60s], and no way could I have been out back then." But that doesn't explain why so many other gay men felt safe enough to come out during those times. The full explanation is missing. As you'll see in the next chapter, a man can have many reasons not to come out that may be just as important, if not more important, than the fear of social stigma.

Often, he's unconsciously aware that if he does come out of the closet he'll have to deal with other psychological "dust bunnies" that he has swept under the rug—issues like finding his authentic self and dealing with family traumas and issues.

Clients like Nick criticize the gay community and sometimes even make homophobic remarks about Gay Pride events. "Why do *we* have to have a parade? Straight people don't need parades." I respond by asking, "Do you feel the same way about the St. Patrick's Day Parade, or the Jewish Walk for Israel, or the various ethnic festivals we have here in Detroit?"

They usually say no, adding, "But that's different. Those festivities aren't about sexuality." Nor are Gay Pridefests. Yes, some of the men dress in drag or leather, but don't marchers in the Irish parades and ethnic festivals also wear their ethnic "drag"?

This is simply a negative filter imprinted early in childhood upon us gay men. There's a whole culture for us to celebrate, honor, and witness just as these other events and festivities do.

Internalized homophobia is very common. Again, this process is unconscious, we're not aware of it. From infancy, we're handed messages that being gay is "wrong" and "bad." So many gay men (and lesbians too) believe the myths and lies perpetuated by heterosexuals—and by gays and lesbians as well!

Then one day—usually in our early teens—we discover that our true, authentic nature is the very thing we've been taught to loathe. We take the homophobia that's been drummed into us and direct it inward, toward ourselves. Again and again in my office, I see the harm and destruction that result when gay men can't accept who they are and—worse yet—judge themselves and others by heterosexual standards. This internalized homophobia often compels gay men to be cruel to themselves and one another.

Psychology 101 teaches the concepts of projection and transference. *Projection* means to assign your own characteristics to other parties in your life. It can be both positive and negative. We constantly make up stories—often, total fantasies—about other people's thoughts, motivations, and intentions. Only rarely do we stop for verification or give others a chance to tell us who they really are. We think we know a person, and there it ends. Problem is, our story is often more about us than about anyone else.

Back when I was taking an Imago relationship training course for therapists, I was shocked to hear of a woman who, after 30 years of marriage, was just beginning to discover who her husband really was! Until then, she'd been making up stories about her spouse—few of them accurate! She'd assumed that her unspoken opinions and judgments corresponded to his feelings and experiences.

Her stories about him were really about her. Whenever she felt down in the dumps, she believed that he didn't respect her "moods" and couldn't tolerate her depressions. Not so! He was simply trying to cheer her up and help her feel better, always with the best of intentions. Her projections arose from her belief that if he really loved her, he'd respond to her in certain ways. This is "magical thinking"—the belief that others will know what we want without our telling them. It was the woman's responsibility to tell her husband that she needed to work through her depressions on her own.

We're born into a culture that generally encourages negative projections toward gay men. Tell some heterosexuals that you're gay and they automatically imagine you in bed with another man and then accuse you of putting your sexuality in their face! But this is projection: They're blaming you for "making" them imagine your sexual behavior.

A school principal once invited me to give a presentation on homosexuality to a group of teachers in his school system. They knew I was coming and understood the topic I was going to present. Afterward, I learned that some teachers had been so upset that they'd stopped listening—or even walked out—simply because I talked about my partner. They felt it was "inappropriate" for me to talk about my "personal" life and that I'd been "preachy" to talk about him and to stick my "gayness" in their face. All I'd done was refer to Mike, naturally and honestly, as an important part of my life as a gay man. If a heterosexual male referred to his wife or girlfriend, people would not get up and leave the room! They'd never accuse the speaker of pushing his sex life in their faces.

Judgments are an inescapable part of daily life. But for gay men, judgment often spells danger, since we're usually judged unworthy as soon as we reveal who we really are. The accumulative effect of these negative judgments takes a toll on our lives. But at the same time, they can contain valuable insights that we shouldn't overlook.

I agree with the client who told me, "Our creator gave us two ears and one mouth, so we can listen twice as much as we talk!" This concept is easy to grasp, but hard to put into practice. It demands that you stop pointing your finger at other parties and ask what your reactions—especially when they're out of proportion to the situation—say about you.

If you react strongly to people who behave in certain ways or say certain things, your reaction says more about you than about those to whom you're reacting. In fact, about 90% of any exaggerated reaction is about yourself.

Big reactions are appropriate to phenomena like gay bashing, the Holocaust, child molestation, and serial killers. However, if someone cuts you off in traffic and you give him the finger, your response is out of proportion to the situation. Maybe the driver didn't see you or really didn't mean to cut you off. Irritation is appropriate. Being outraged and even vengeful is overreacting.

Transference means to take the positive and negative traits of significant, influential people in our lives and unconsciously transfer them onto somebody else—usually one's partner, friend, colleagues, or therapist. Usually the people we feel closest to. We professionals actually hope for this! We want clients to transfer their feelings onto us so we can help them see the issues they have with other people in their lives, resolve them, and move on.

Imago Relationship Therapists understand that in relationships this phenomenon is normal. We try to help couples understand that partners do engage in transference with one another and that it's usually a positive indicator they're in a healthy relationship.

No one is free from projection, transference, or judgments. The crucial issue is to learn how to deal with them. Judgments are not innately "bad." You can use them in very effective ways once you accept that your reactions are your own and that they tell you a lot more about yourself than about the people you judge.

Our gay and lesbian culture is under constant assault. Virtually every day, some newspaper article or TV program takes issue with somebody who's openly, visibly gay. The Boy Scouts don't want us in their troops, the Pentagon doesn't want us in their Army or Navy, and churches don't want us in the pulpit.

What's the best way to stand up to bigotry? Every gay man who reads this book should resolve to stop feeling like a victim and to become an empowered adult. Yes, societal problems do exist. We all have to combat insults, offenses, and tragedies. But first, start to work on yourself, as an individual. Only after you determine the psychological effects of cultural abuse can you lay those issues to rest and move ahead with your life.

Only then can you be an effective activist on behalf of our gay brothers and sisters.

Psychologist Carl G. Jung coined the term "shadow" to describe the parts of one's self that are repressed, undeveloped, or denied. He taught that if we are in shadow, we project denied aspects of ourselves onto others. Inner dynamics "in shadow" are ones you're not consciously aware of, but which nonetheless run at full speed!

Contrary to popular belief, your shadow can be positive as well as negative. Yes, if repressed, it can wreak considerable damage. But as soon as you recognize and accept it, it can be a source of tremendous psychological wealth.

Robert Bly, a respected poet, is best known for his groundbreaking men's movement best-seller, *Iron John*. In his later book, *A Little Book on the Human Shadow*, he discusses how projections bleed away your personal energy.[1] In other words, when you ascribe your own best qualities and character traits to others, you deny and deplete them in yourself. I couldn't agree more! The very traits you strongly dislike—or like, for that matter—in others (including straight society) usually reflect some unresolved issue lurking inside you.

For example, if you idealize another person and therefore overreact to them, you may overlook positive aspects of that person reflected in you. Similarly, if you focus on hating others' behavior or character traits, you won't have the knowledge to deal with those same defects in yourself.

We diminish ourselves by staying in shadow. Whenever a client overreacts to some "outside" issue in his life, I see it as a signal that he's really talking about himself, in some not-so-indirect way.

I maintain a large mailing list that goes out to thousands of people, gay and straight alike. When I did my first mailing to advertise my gay men's group therapy and weekend workshops, I just thumbed through phone books, scanned for local gay listings and gay-friendly businesses, and compiled a mailing list of about 500 addresses.

I printed up a batch of one-page flyers, trifolded them, and affixed a sticker to make sure they'd stay shut. I added a stamp, my return address, and a forwarding request, and dumped them in a mailbox. I figured that if the recipients weren't interested in my flyer, they would simply toss it or pass it along to a friend.

By then, I had been openly gay for 12 years. I'd grown quite distant from the kind of homophobia I was about to face. Following the mailing, I received several heartening calls from men in the Detroit area, eager to join a gay men's group. But other callers were outraged, asking "How dare you send me this mailing about a gay group with no envelope?" If they were closeted, they might have feared their child, husband, or wife would see my flyer and connect the dots. Others were simply annoyed at my presumption that they were gay. Would they have been offended if I presumed they were straight?

Every year I receive thousands of letters about Attention Deficit Disorder, menopause, diabetes, and rape. I never worry how these senders single me out. I never take offense, but lots of others do—if they get mail dealing with gay and lesbian subject matter.

Most of those who overreact in this way are in their own

shadows. My mailings simply inflame their own inner conflicts. All too vividly I recall what I endured during my adolescence and young adulthood with therapists who were anything but gay-affirmative. I'd have come out earlier but for these well-intentioned therapists who wanted to "change" me into a heterosexual. I determined not to let homophobic reactions stop me from providing—and promoting—effective, supportive therapy to our gay brothers and sisters.

I hope that while reading this book, you'll identify your own projections, transference, shadows, and judgments. Reclaim the good in yourself that you've been overlooking or giving away. Increasing your self-awareness and taking responsibility for your own life are the only (certainly the fastest!) ways to achieve personal freedom as a gay man. Becoming accountable for your own words and actions is what integrity and responsibility are all about. If you remain focused on what other people do and say—or *won't* do or say—that means asking them to be responsible and accountable for your own happiness. Surrendering your own welfare into their hands will only leave you angry and empty, a hostage to what others want—or expect you to be.

References

1. Robert Bly, *A Little Book on the Human Shadow*. New York: HarperCollins Publishers (1988).

Chapter 2
Affirm Yourself by Coming Out

IT IS BETTER TO BE HATED FOR WHO YOU ARE,
THAN TO BE LOVED FOR WHO YOU ARE NOT.
—Andre Gide

The first step to living a full life—coming out of the closet—is no small task. Society accepts that women can be very close friends, enjoy deeply meaningful relationships, and express their affection in loving language. Today, Oprah Winfrey frequently talks about her best friend, Gail. They're never accused of being lovers. But when Ben Affleck and Matt Damon talk about being best friends and attend social events together, people suspect they're romantically and sexually involved.

When he sees teachers, parents, and other authority figures practice homophobia and heterosexism, the gay young boy learns to hide. Actually, hiding can be a smart move on his part, because being out—in the wrong place, at an inappropriate time—can mean ostracism, abuse, and even physical and psychological injury. Gay male teens often have to pretend to be something they're not. They must make many decisions, consciously and unconsciously, about how to deal with their homosexuality.

In my years as a psychotherapist I've met many gay men who were shamed into hiding, marrying, and even raising children. Some say they honestly did not know they were gay. They always state that their intentions were honorable and that they hoped their homosexual leanings would somehow "go away."

Ironically, when these men can no longer live their lives in hiding, conservative people blame *them* for coming out and ask, "If you knew you were gay, why did you marry in the first place? How could you do this to your wife and kids?"

Beginning the coming-out process triggers many different life events. Generally, when a woman has sex with another women, she begins to consider the possibility that she's a lesbian. Society permits a woman to love other women openly and affectionately, but it's taboo for her to be sexual with another woman, unless she's performing for a straight man's entertainment and arousal.

By contrast, men often have sex with other men without labeling their experience homosexuality. Instead they can keep it secret and deny it. They may go to a public park, hire an escort, or have a self-identified gay man service them orally—and then forget about it so they don't have to deal with their difficult feelings. Not until they fall in love with another man do they begin to consider that they might be gay. Powerful emotions like love are just harder to deny.

Victor, a successful 25-year-old car salesman with a wife and two preschool-age twins, came to therapy because he'd discovered he was gay. Until recently, he reported, the thought of being gay had never entered his mind. He'd had close male friends and never questioned his feelings for them. He'd never had any sexual encounters with them, though he'd had some sexual fantasies of being with other men. But he just figured everyone had them and decided not to give them too much thought. He was happily married and loved being a husband and father—until he went on a sales trip in a neighboring state.

On the plane, the man in the next seat struck up a conversation. Unsure at first what was happening, Vic found himself sexually attracted and thought the feeling was mutual. When they landed, Andy gave Vic his card and told him what hotel he was in. After checking in, Vic couldn't get his mind off Andy. He went to his presentation and, that evening, found himself compelled to call

Andy. Over dinner, Andy admitted that he was gay and wanted to have sex with Vic, who couldn't believe his ears. For the first time in his life, began to wonder if he was gay. He was strongly attracted to Andy in many ways—not just sexually.

That night, he accepted Andy's invitation. Never had Vic had a sexual experience so good, right, and exciting! After the trip he returned home, riddled with guilt.

Cheating was not part of his value system. Yet he felt a call from deep inside himself; separate from his marriage. Vic and Andy kept in touch over the phone and found they had lots in common. Vic was falling in love with Andy. Andy eventually joined him on another business trip. After their week together, Vic knew, without doubt, that he was in love—and that he was gay.

His tension, guilt, and emotional devastation were overwhelming. What would he do? His twins had just turned three. What about his marriage? Though divorce wasn't part of his value system, it tortured him to be dishonest. Vic decided to come out of the closet. These details, his attorney warned, could only work against visitation rights.

His wife, parents, and in-laws were enraged. All of them asked him the same question: How could he marry, knowing he was gay? No one believed his assertion that he hadn't known. Once Andy walked into his life, he confessed, the floodgates opened, confirming his real identity.

Vic's wife tried to use his homosexuality as grounds to deny him contact with their toddlers. The judge dismissed her motion. Not all gay men are so lucky.

Vic and the other men I've treated have actually not been bisexual. When I ask, they tell me that women don't excite them sexually. They could perform sexually with their wives because they loved them. But no other women caught their gaze. In the well-known prison syndrome, inmates have sex with other men—even fall in love with them—but they aren't bisexual. Upon their release, they return to strict heterosexual behavior, because that's their orientation.

It takes gay men a while to discover themselves. Even so, boys tend to discover they're gay earlier than girls. Some of my clients report they knew as early as age 3 that they had homosexual feelings, but didn't know what to call them. On average, gay men first become aware of their sexual orientation by age 14, whereas women discover their feelings at 18 years or older.[1]

A boy quickly discovers what's acceptable and what's not. If he tries to dress up Barbies, touch another boy, or play house, he swiftly realizes his impulses and desires are unacceptable. He is usually shamed into stopping the behavior. Girls are given some leeway to play with boys' toys and to join in their sports. They're allowed to have sleepovers and brush each other's hair.

Not all gay boys care to play with girls' toys. In fact, some straight boys do! But the boy drawn to "sissy" behavior learns that something is "different and wrong" with him. During this period of introspection, he discovers his gayness earlier than his lesbian peer.

My heterosexual sister didn't like wearing dresses and identified with boys. We have a snapshot of her playing baseball, holding a bat, and wearing a uniform. We all laugh and say how cute she looked during her tomboy years. For her, it was a stage she grew out of.

In her essay in *Sissies and Tomboys: Gender Nonconformity and Homosexual Childhood,* Diane Elise says, "A tomboy becomes a short-lived, insignificant phase that we ignore or humor out of existence as merely a lapse in the ongoing stream of feminine development."[2] Why, then, do we make such an issue out of sissy boys?

When I was young, I'd put my sister's black tights on my head, wear one of my mother's dresses, pretend I was Cher, and lip-sync to her music. I assure you, there are no family snapshots of Joey's sissy years. That was a stage for me too.

There is no acceptable time period for a young boy to explore his feminine side, because his exploration would call attention to the fact that he might be different. Boys cannot touch one another unless the contact is sports-related, so *wanting* to touch another boy is a red flag. The tendency to break cultural taboos doesn't necessarily indicate a young male's sexual orientation, but it definitely calls for him to become introspective—and to realize that he is different—at an earlier age.

Many clients report "sissy type" histories similar to mine. Nonconformity to gender role expectations doesn't create homosexual orientation, but it is a positive indicator for a gay boy's later development. Similarly, the smothering mother/absent father combination doesn't *make* a boy gay, but is a common parental *reaction* to a son's being gay.

Such experiences force young gay boys into the closet. This means abandoning essential parts of ourselves to conform to social conventions. We repress (an unconscious process) and suppress (consciously) sexual impulses and fantasies. As we mature, we avoid other men who might be gay.

Carl, 31 years old, came to me because he had trouble finding a relationship. He'd been out for 10 years to his friends and family, but couldn't find a partner. He attributed this to his poor self-esteem and believed he "wasn't attractive enough for the gay community."

While exploring his history, it became clear that all the friends to whom he was out were straight. He had no close gay friends at all! Carl was attracted only to younger guys around 20. His pursuits always ended in heartbreak. Young men of that age are emotionally and developmentally different from men of 31.

Why was he so strongly attracted to younger men? I immediately identified his internalized homophobia: He had no supportive gay male friendships because he believed that gay men are all promiscuous.

Carl didn't like being labeled homophobic. On his second visit, he told me he was angry and almost hadn't returned. Over the course of therapy, he saw how some of his actions and thinking were in fact internalized homophobia. Not until he came out of the closet could he have faced this issue.

He began to attend my workshops for gay men, where we examine the impact of internalized homophobia. Carl became more comfortable about his gayness and, while going for his Ph.D. degree, came out to his peers and teachers—something he'd never have done before. He felt much better as an openly gay man and began to talk about leaving therapy. But certain things still bothered him.

He soon realized why he was so attracted to young men of 20.

They were around the age Carl had been when he dropped out of college to avoid pursuing a full gay life. He had suffered for 11 years. On his awakening, he was still 20 years old emotionally.

But that was only part of the story. In our initial sessions, I'd asked Carl about incidents of past abuse. He stated there hadn't been any. As it turned out, he was in denial. An uncle had sexually abused him in childhood. Carl couldn't have tackled this either until he'd worked through the top layers of his coming out and internalized homophobia.

Sexual abuse makes you feel unloved, inherently flawed, unworthy. Carl had packed his experience away in his closet, and he associated being unloved with being gay—the source of his internalized homophobia. He had work to do on his childhood abuse, which involved directly addressing memories he had denied and affirming that what happened to him was wrong.

When gay men are taught to display a false public self and to hide their true feelings, they enter a socialization process all children go through. In a family where parents admonish their son, "Don't be angry," a boy learns to hide his anger, or finds other ways to express it. If a student learns what's appropriate to win social acceptance, he'll conform. We call this peer pressure, and only "geeks" and "nerds" who are socially "out of it" are immune. But gays and lesbians have an additional task—to publicly display heterosexuality. Their core sexual and romantic identity is buried, along with the other traits necessary to build social skills.

In *Keeping the Love You Find: A Guide for Singles*, Harville Hendrix speaks about the social journey we all must take to develop our sense of self.[3] We're born with most of our thinking, feeling, and sensory functions intact. In a healthy family, parents send messages that it's OK to be you, to experience all of your body senses, to have feelings and express them, to solve problems, to be assertive. But that's not always what happens. Instead, we often get conflicting messages.

The messages we accept—or choose to obey—help to determine our place in the family we grow up in—even the culture we live in.

Hendrix says that people develop a "fugitive self" that goes underground, where even heterosexuals sometimes have to hide. Because we want our parents and primary caretakers to return our love, we decide—in our childhood brilliance—to lose those potentially troublemaking aspects of ourselves and to pretend they aren't there. Of course, they're not really gone for good, but they're certainly out of our conscious scrutiny. I use Hendrix's ideas in my workshops to emphasize how gay men's core sexual identity gets buried along with any other "unacceptable" and "unfashionable" traits.

Like Carl, all of us develop a lost or denied self. In essence, a person hides who he really is and presents a false self to the world. Eventually, he believes the lie himself.

In a fortunately rare medical disorder, the "sufferer" cannot experience physical pain in their limbs. Nerve receptors meant to send physical-distress messages to the brain cease to function properly. Wouldn't it be nice to be forever relieved of aches and pains? No! Horrified parents find afflicted children finger-painting in their own blood or a man steps on a nail which scratches the bone and he does not feel it until infection sets in and the limb needs to be removed. We *need* pain to avoid injury and signal that we need medical attention.

You see the parallel: The lost and denied self cannot "feel" whatever threatens it—and by extension, the individual as a whole—until it's too late. First, we consciously suppress these parts of ourselves as foreign to us. Then we *un*consciously repress them—so that they become literally "out of sight."

For example: A mother warns her daughter, "Don't act too smart, or boys won't be attracted to you." That girl grows up not believing herself intelligent, when of course she is.

Similarly, a boy who is told not to sit or stand or walk in certain ways loses touch with his own body. The boy becomes a gay man who's clueless about his urges.

The aspects of personality "lost," denied, and suppressed are different for everyone. Lost for all closeted gay men, however, is the possibility of romantic and sexual relationship. "The longer you stay inside your closet," I remind clients, "the more it transforms into a coffin, where only death exists. There's no room to grow."

To disguise their authentic selves, gay men spend enormous amounts of time throwing others off track. This destructive expenditure of energy can lead to panic disorders, erectile difficulty, drug and alcohol abuse, sexual addiction and compulsivity, sexual anorexia (a total shutdown of libido), even suicide attempts.

At least 30% of teenagers who attempt suicide do so because they are struggling with sexual identity. In cases like Carl's where childhood sexual abuse is a factor, when the perpetrator is the same gender as the victim, the boy wonders, "Am I gay or straight? Did I make that happen?"

Harry, a 34-year-old single office manager, complained of asexuality—he had no desire for either gender. The very thought of being sexual at all—even masturbation—caused nausea and extreme psychological discomfort. His primary care physician had ruled out any medical disorder.

Harry identified with much of what he read in Patrick Carnes's *Sexual Anorexia*.[4] He'd never thought of himself as gay or straight, had never had a romantic love relationship, and had been sexual with only a few men and women. He enjoyed both, but found himself bothered by—and ashamed of—his gay encounters. Harry constantly worried that others might think he was gay. Also HIV-phobic, he refused to have gay roommates—over his fear that people would label him as gay and that he would contract AIDS from them in nonsexual ways.

In our work, Harry discovered that he was avoiding others, sexually and socially, to avoid addressing his core orientation. He agreed to attend one of my men's sexuality therapy groups. Harry's isolation made it hard for him to get close to other group members—participants said they "felt a distance" from him.

In the group, Harry became increasingly uncomfortable. He also attended my workshops, where he identified himself as bisexual. Repeatedly he objected to the workshops' structure, the seating arrangements, and the hours involved. Later, in therapy, he agreed that these trivial complaints were simply outlets for his discomfort at being with other gay men. All weekend long, he worried that someone he knew would see him entering the building where the workshop was taking place.

After six months of both group and individual work, Harry chose not to continue to try to resolve his sexual orientation. He confessed that he was most comfortable being alone, and that therapy only made him more anxious. At this time, he wasn't ready or willing to do more. As a group, we all honored his decision. Men deserve the right to find their own way at their own pace.

I often tell the following joke at my workshops: A man asks a tailor to make him a suit. After being measured, he leaves and returns a week later—to find that one sleeve of the jacket is too short. The tailor tells him, "Bend your arm and raise your shoulder. Now it fits perfectly."

"But the other sleeve's too long."

Again, the tailor suggests that he bend and raise his arm. The sleeve fits perfectly! "What about the pants?" the client asks. "One leg's longer than the other."

The tailor shows him how to adjust his legs up and down until the suit fits perfectly. He's now twisted like a pretzel—but his suit fits like a glove! He pays the tailor and walks off down the street.

Two women see him hobbling. One says, "What a wonderful tailor, to make a fine suit for such a crippled man!"

Gay men are told to put on a suit that doesn't fit us, and we gamely try to pretend that it does. Others call us "crippled," so we begin to think we really are. But there's nothing wrong with us; what's wrong is what has been done *to* us. We need to take off the psychological suits that others have assigned us and begin to see ourselves without shame. And we need to find another tailor!

How do we do this? By coming out.

Many of my clients decide to be out in various—usually limited—ways. Some are out only to themselves and to me. Much of this reticence is justified: As media stories of gay bashings attest, coming out in the wrong place at the wrong time can have grave consequences. But in places where men may safely come out without putting at risk their jobs or physical safety, learning to live outside the closet is essential.

Many gay men I've worked with say they want to come out, but they don't think it's necessary to tell everyone what they do sexually. "Others don't need to know my sex life," they often say. I point out that being gay isn't just about sexuality. Even if gays and lesbians were celibate, they'd still be gay or lesbian. If a man's going to come out, he must recognize his act isn't an admission of what he does sexually but an affirmation of who he is romantically, spiritually, emotionally, and psychologically.

Some clients don't feel the need to come out to their family or friends. "They already know," some say. I challenge them: "Then what's the risk in telling?" Even if these people *do* know, why not be open? Often clients say they don't need to tell, because "Straight people don't tell me they're straight!" I reply that straight people don't have to out themselves formally.

Heterosexism simply assumes that everyone is straight until proven otherwise. Straight people talk openly about their spouses, their girlfriends and boyfriends, and the singles bars they frequent. If a gay client omits this kind of information, I usually suspect internalized homophobia.

Many clients say, "I'm waiting for Mr. Right. Then I'll have a reason to come out." To which I reply, "Why aren't *you* Mr. Right Enough? What can waiting for another man possibly do for you?" We explore how this is a rationalization, a psychological defense to postpone coming out. What's more, this strategy reduces a client's chances of ever finding a partner.

Gays and lesbians who desire to be partnered before coming out often want to emulate the heterosexual world, where being half of a couple is valued more than being single. For many gay men, being single is yet another blow to self-esteem. When Rosie O'Donnell came out on *Prime Time Live*, Diane Sawyer asked, "Why come out now?" "I wanted to wait until I was in a long-term committed relationship," Rosie said. Many gays and lesbians feel more empowered under these conditions.

What can gay men expect when they begin the coming-out

process? Vivienne C. Cass's *Model of Homosexuality Identity Formation*[5] best reflects my own process of coming out and the stages I've observed in my clients.

Stage One: Identity Confusion

According to Cass, the first step is *coming out to yourself.* During this stage a man begins to notice, recognize, and acknowledge his own sexual attraction to other men. Men don't see themselves as even remotely gay; they still identify themselves as heterosexual. This isn't role-playing—they honestly believe they are straight.

In my years of practice, I've met many clients who worry they may be gay, because they have same-sex fantasies or even encounters. But merely wondering whether one is gay or having sexual contact with another man is not necessarily stage one of coming out. There are a number of things to rule in and to rule out. The fantasy or behavior might be a manifestation of childhood sexual abuse by a male perpetrator. Or it could be an escalation of sexual addiction, where the "taboo" homosexual behavior affords an added thrill. Some bisexual or bi-attractional tendencies have nothing to do with one's core sexual identity.

This is the stage where many psychotherapists can do harm. Most don't even know about the stages of coming out. Many try to reassure their clients by offering all kinds of explanations for homosexual behavior. They often overlook the possibility that their client is beginning the process of self-recognition that will reveal his gay identity. I think it's important to go further and inform clients that homosexual sex can mean a lot of things—including the possibility that they're at stage one of the coming-out process. But because this causes so much discomfort for many men, therapists' good intentions (and often, their own homophobia) prompt them to steer clients—particularly male adolescents—away from such thoughts.

Many therapists have told me they're reluctant to educate a teen about homosexuality for fear that he'll become excessively upset or wonder why his therapist is examining this area. They usually report to me that in their attempt not to overload a client—teen or otherwise—

they "let those thoughts go their own course" and don't fully explore them. Some well-meaning therapists don't explore them at all and even avoid the client's expressions of same-sex desires.

I think this kind of avoidance itself is harmful. I usually tell a client, "There are a number of possibilities here." If the man is struggling with his feelings for men, I don't push the word *gay* because I believe it's an affirmative word that defines an entire way of life—including romantic, spiritual, psychological, and sexual connection to other men. Many men have homosexual desires, but are strictly "hetero-emotional." Although they are sexually attracted to men, they are romantically interested in women only.

After I have taken a thorough history of the client's background and educated him about the stages of coming out, the client can then make his own decision. It's arrogant for us therapists to decide for a client who he is or isn't, or who he should or shouldn't be.

Also during this undecided first stage, men begin to consider going to reparative therapies that propose to "cure" homosexuality. In my view, men who pursue this option do a lot of damage to their self-esteem, and consequently to their lives. I ask clients to consider that there's nothing to cure. They might decide not to act on their homosexual desires or ever to come out—that's their decision. In my therapeutic judgment, homosexual feelings don't need to be "cured" or "repaired."

Stage Two: Identity Comparison

During this stage, a man begins to accept the possibility that he might be homosexual. Again, he would not use the word *gay*, because of its association with a particular way of life. *Homosexual* is simply a word he can use to start exploring sexual feelings from a "safe" distance.

In Stage Two of the coming-out process, men begin to feel positive about being different. They might also accept their *behavior* as homosexual, while they still reject homosexuality as their core identity. Last, they might accept their identity, but inhibit their homosexual or gay behavior—by deciding to marry a woman or by having anonymous "no strings" sex, for example.

It's here that psychotherapists—gay and lesbian therapists in particular—do damage by forcing the issue. After exploring homosexuality, some people may decide it's not for them. Their decision isn't a product of shame or guilt. These clients don't see homosexuality that needs to be cured or fixed. Instead, they simply discover they're not connecting to a gay identity. Just like adults who, having been raised Jewish or Catholic, decide to change religions, they must decide on the identity that fits them best.

Yes, I realize I'm treading on thin ice. Many would accuse me of helping people live a life fraught with depression, which, according to the American Psychological Association, is the usual fate of those who live a closeted life. I agree with the APA, but as a Gay Affirmative Psychotherapist, it's my job to help clients feel good about their homosexual feelings and gay identity. And to help people become who *they* want to be, not who I think they should be.

If a client committed to Reparative Therapy asked to see me, I'd tell him I view that therapy as abusive and refer him elsewhere. However, I have supported some men who decided for themselves that a homosexual identity wasn't for them and planned to enter a heterosexual marriage. My coaching here usually involved educating them about life in the closet and about the APA's warnings. To help them make an informed choice, I explain that they needn't feel wrong or bad for having these feelings. That is where we should ground any important life decision. I also coach these men to be forthcoming with any women with whom they might become involved.

Darryl, 36 years old, came to me depressed about his job situation. His company had just been bought out, and his new boss had increased his workload. He had been heterosexually married, with no children, for nearly 14 years, and he loved his wife deeply. At his workplace, he told his Employee Assistance Personnel (EAP) counselor about his homosexual feelings. Knowing that I specialized in issues involving homosexuality, she referred him to me.

Darryl stated he'd "acted out" homosexually during his late teens—before meeting his current wife—and reported feeling a lot of shame about it. Over the years, he'd worked with many different therapists, all of whom informed him that his feelings were rooted in his unsatisfying relationship with his father. According to these therapists, Darryl had sexualized his desire for a strong father figure. In his primarily heterosexual therapy groups, these therapists told him to keep his homosexual feelings to himself, lest he suffer the negative feedback and judgments from his peers within the group.

Darryl complied. He didn't share much with his therapists because they simply told him, "If you don't give your feelings much energy, they will go away." They never did, of course, and Darryl was ashamed of this part of himself and saw it as a pathology.

Before making the referral, his EAP had already told Darryl I was gay. When I asked if that was a problem, Darryl said, "No. Maybe looking at this from a gay person's point of view for a change might help."

During our work together, Darryl was finally able to talk at length about his sexuality. He told me he could have enjoyable and satisfying sexual relations with his wife. He was able to be 100% fully engaged with her and didn't think about men or other women. (Many self-identified gay men confess they have to think of men while having intercourse with a woman.) Darryl did say that other women didn't excite him in the least. He was always sexually drawn to men and had had all of his other sexual experiences with men.

Darryl felt his homosexual impulses were something to be ashamed of and indicated that he was "less of a man." His parents would often compare him unfavorably to other males. Darryl was convinced this had led to his homosexual feelings—and his previous therapists supported his conclusion. While I can see how this experience could lead a client to eroticize males, I didn't think this was true for Darryl. He was sexually drawn to men, and not at all to women. Again, his romantic attraction to his wife led to a sexual arousal and positive experience. In other words, while Daryll was not sexually attracted to women, his wife could sexually satisfy him because he was romantically connected to her.

Significantly, women often report that this is true for them as well: They're attracted to a man romantically and their sexual feelings are secondary. They often state that they need romance in order to feel sexual.

Darryl could never imagine being in a relationship with another man. Unable to be romantic with men, he'd be unfulfilled in any gay relationship. He was "shocked" to learn I had been with my partner for so long (at that time, about six years) and even more shocked to learn I planned to marry him. He often told me he thought I was "playing house" and only "kidding myself" when I said I had a good life.

This is an example of negative transference; Because Darryl didn't believe he could have a fulfilling gay life, he pushed his negative beliefs about homosexuality onto me.

He entered a men's sexuality group I facilitated that included gay, bisexual, and straight men. For the first time, Darryl heard gay men speak about loving, caring, intimate relationships in a positive, healthy light. Still, he still felt that his own sexual feelings for men reflected his low self-esteem. He didn't identify himself as gay and interpreted his homoeroticism as a form of pathology.

Over five years of therapy with me, both individually and in group, his negative feelings about his homosexuality lessened. Eventually, he told his wife that I, his therapist, was gay. I thought this might be a prelude to his finally telling her about himself. He reported that she was tolerant and accepting of gay men when he raised the topic, but he didn't believe that she would be OK with his having the same impulses.

Darryl had never acted on those impulses during his marriage. What a tribute to his wife that he remained faithful! Many group members praised him for being faithful and showing integrity, but he couldn't take that in. To accept it would mean honoring himself as a man, which went against the messages his parents had given him—that he was not a "real man."

I believe it's important for partners to be able to tell their significant others who they are, so I coached Darryl to consider telling his wife about his sexual feelings for men. Otherwise, he was hiding an important part of himself. He resisted telling her because he didn't want to leave her, to be sexual with men, or to "come out." None of that fit him. He worried she'd think that he wanted out of the marriage or would leave her after his confession.

Darryl agreed to attend my gay men's workshop, and he threw himself into the exercises. After completing the entire weekend and returning to group therapy, he began self-identifying as bisexual. He grew more comfortable with his sexual feelings for men.

Finally, he decided to tell his wife. His effort at honesty was a success. Although shocked, his wife honored his bravery and his commitment to their marriage. His depression lifted, his self-esteem improved, and his therapy was complete. Darryl is an example of a man who stopped at the second stage of the coming-out process and decided to stay married to the woman he loved. He'd accepted the homosexual part of his identity but inhibited his behavior.

Darryl, I believe, is both hetero-emotional and homosexual. I think that if homophobic therapists hadn't told him that his feelings stemmed from an eroticized father figure—and if he had had a more positive exposure to gay culture—Darryl might have realized that he was OK and accepted his homosexual feelings earlier. In any case, what's important is that he's living the life *he* wants to live. He needed to remove the stigma from his feelings for men and claim his birthright to have complex sexual feelings.

Unfortunately, during the second stage many gay men choose to seek reparative therapies. The hate and negativity that advocates of these therapies attach to being gay only further shames a man into believing his condition is "wrong." Reparative therapists don't offer a balanced approach to helping men make educated, self-affirming decisions. It's simply not healthy to devalue one's gayness, which poses serious consequences to one's self-esteem.

Stage Three: Identity Tolerance

Here, the individual accepts the likelihood that he is homosexual and begins to move toward using the word *gay* to describe himself. This isn't the case for those who decide not to continue their coming-out process. While Darryl was in stage two, for example, he did not identify as being gay. At stage three, the client begins to consider a homosexual identity—trying it on, to see whether it fits. He may still hesitate to venture into the gay culture. Bad experiences might push him to decide that although he accepts himself as gay, he doesn't want to live openly.

Ahmed was a 24-year-old chef's apprentice, living at home with his widowed Algerian mother. He was very self-conscious about his dark skin and premature hair loss. He had identified himself as gay for some time but was having many bad experiences as he tried to enter the gay community. Men at gay bars were judgmental about his heavy Algerian accent. Some men he approached even told him that his hair loss made him unattractive.

At the gay community center, Ahmed found that people were equally aloof. Despite these setbacks, he felt the need to out himself—to venture into the straight world as a self-identified gay man. Toward this end he adopted a screen name with "gay" in it and entered online chat rooms that were mainly heterosexual. Intellectually, he knew this was a virtual experience and that people did not really know him, but the emotions Ahmed felt were very real. Unkind chatters typed sarcastic comments like, "Men4Men room down the hall," or "No fudgepackers allowed here."

One of the psychological benefits of chat rooms is that they let people reveal themselves as they really are and say whatever they want. As I listened to Ahmed, I realized that his foray into the online straight world was great practice for him! He learned to respond in a healthy way to the beliefs of heterosexists while remaining anonymous.

Another factor that brought Ahmed to treatment was his family's opposition to his being gay. Clients and students have warned me that in Islamic cultures it's not safe to be out.

Ahmed had met many other Arabic men who were closeted and who would not socialize with other gay men outside of all-gay functions. This consistent denial turned Ahmed off to other Arabic men and to gay life. In the gay community, in the chat rooms, and in his family, all of his experiences had been negative. As a last resort, he decided to enter therapy with me. "If this doesn't work," he confessed, "I might closet myself for the rest of my life."

In Ahmed's view, the gay community was superficial and overly sexual, and the straight community was generally unfriendly and often hostile. The Talmud has a wise saying: "We see the world as we are, not as it is." Ahmed viewed everything from his own limited perspective.

There is no *one* gay or straight community. Each community has many facets. You can find what you are looking for, but you must persevere. That was the essence of my coaching to Ahmed—to help him find the right places for him. For starters, I said that for him, the bars were out!

Straight or gay, bars are usually where people look for Mr. Right Now, not Mr. Right. Generally speaking, the bar scene is one big high school—developmentally and emotionally, everyone's about 16 years old. Which isn't to say that bars don't have their time and place. I prompt many clients to go to bars socially, for a good time. They meet someone? Fine! A few men have met lifetime partners at bars, but I coach them not to expect to.

Ahmed came to my gay men's workshops. As a "good son," Ahmed found the parts of the workshop relating to family very difficult. The hardest part for him was fear of letting his family down. He knew they would never fully approve of him, would have to go through a grieving process, and would have to admit they were the mother and siblings of a gay son and brother—something not acceptable in their culture. He made strong friendships at the workshop and even dated some of the men after the weekend. His self-esteem went up, and these positive experiences helped move Ahmed toward an affirmative acceptance of his gay self.

Returning to the gay community center, he found more people with whom he could relate. Yes, some men there still judged him for his "baldness and heavy accent." But he was able to overlook this and approach men who weren't judgmental. Ahmed then moved toward the next stage of coming out.

Stage Four: Identity Acceptance

This is the movement from simple tolerance to accepting—and identifying—oneself as gay. Now the individual discovers a new sense of belonging, seeking how to fit into the gay community as a whole. He feels increasing anger at the antigay segments of society—and this is healthy too! He takes all the doubt and self-hatred he used to direct inward and diverts it outward, at more deserving targets.

Again, as a healthy reaction, he distances himself from people and places that would disrupt his new way of thinking and his new self-acceptance. This is very similar to the adolescent male who, having gone through puberty, starts identifying with his growing sexuality. And, just as teenagers experience an acute need for privacy, he distances himself from his family. He keeps his door closed, adopts music and fashions (which he knows his parents won't like) to set himself apart from them, and bonds with his peers, who recognize his newfound sexual self. Few parents are delighted when a teenager goes through this stage, but school counselors and therapists normalize this process. It's a passing stage, necessary for the teen to get a sense of belonging and forge a personal identity.

This is appropriate—nothing to worry about. Similarly, Gay Affirmative Psychotherapy sees identity acceptance as normal for individuals of any age. Like an adolescent accepting his new identity, a gay man may well choose new friends and hangouts to shield himself from any negative views about his homosexuality—or anyone else's. Gay Affirmative Psychotherapy honors this stage as developmentally appropriate.

Stage Five: Identity Pride

The next stage even more closely parallels the stages of adolescent development. Here, the individual totally accepts his own self-image, even as he becomes equally aware of society's rejection of it. To bridge this dilemma, the gay man will reinforce, even emphasize, the differences between being gay and being straight. A teenager might dye his hair blue, pierce his body, and horrify his parents with "outrageous" behavior. The gay man might plaster his car with rainbow stickers, vacation in San Francisco or Key West, and out himself to everyone in his life.

All his previous repression is now explosively directed outward.

This is when he wants to go on *Oprah* and come out to the world. He'll read only gay literature, devouring all aspects and trademarks of the gay culture. He starts to disdain the heterosexual world—now it's "them against us."

This stage creates the best activists! His combination of anger and pride spark the gay man to become heavily, passionately involved in gay rights organizations and gay pride marches. On the downside, this is where this same man might be judged as "too" gay. (In 1997, Ellen DeGeneres decided to come out—personally and in character—on her hit television show, *Ellen*. The remainder of the series was an illustration of identity pride, centering for the most part on gay issues. Even gay people accused both Ellen and *Ellen* of being "too gay.")

It's important to recognize Identity Pride. In my office, I often see men upward of 50 years old. They wear T-shirts saying I CAN'T EVEN THINK STRAIGHT, sport a gay pride rainbow hat, or drive to my office in a rainbow-plastered car.

They often proclaim that they're gay and proud, even if they feel a little foolish acting out in this manner at their age. They don't yet fully understand their own behavior. Also, there's tremendous grief inside them—they wish they'd made this change earlier in life and sometimes mistake their behavior for a "midlife" crisis. I reframe it for them as a life awakening and educate them on the stages of coming out. I reassure them that they're just in the "gay adolescent" stage of Identity Pride—a necessary step for their self-actualization as gay men. Almost always, they breathe a sigh of relief when they learn there's a name for their experience.

Clients are sometimes afraid to achieve this stage—or afraid they'll get stuck in it. "I don't want to become the type of gay man who waves a rainbow flag around." While I reassure them that doesn't have to happen, I also explore their potential homophobia: What's wrong with a little flamboyance?

When I returned home from the 1993 Gay Pride March on Washington, many gay friends—and clients—were angry that the television news media focused mostly on the "drag queens, leather queens, and rainbow-waving activists."

"Did you go?" I'd ask.

"I'd never be caught dead there," was the common response.

Many clients are frustrated that heterosexual society focuses only on the transgendered and "Wigstock" drag queens, not on gay men who look ordinary. Still, those queens and activists were brave enough to get out there and fight for the rest of us.

The final stage of the coming-out process is:

Stage Six: Identity Synthesis

At this stage of integration, the concept of "them and us" is no longer useful. The gay man begins to understand that not all heterosexuals are antigay. Like an older adolescent, he can relax his militant stance and reintegrate himself with the whole of society. He understands that heterosexism and homophobia exist, and that there's a power imbalance in the world, but this state of affairs does not dominate his life. He can relate to both gays and straights without losing his self-confidence.

Coming out is a lifelong process; it never ends. Cass's six stages describe a step-by-step process, but every man is different. Clients veer back and forth, through all the stages. Some men come out to an increasing number of people at different stages of their lives. When I first came out to myself, I looked up the word "homosexual" in library books and all the textbooks we used in high school. Then, during my teen years, I came out all over again to therapists. I came out to my family, then to my friends in college. But I didn't come out professionally until 1988. Each new day provides a fresh chance to progress in this journey.

References

1. Peg Hanley-Hackenbruck, M.D., "Psychotherapy and the 'Coming Out' Process," in *Journal of Gay and Lesbian Psychotherapy*, Vol. 1 (1), 1989.

2. Diane Elise, "Tomboys and Cowgirls," in *Sissies and Tomboys: Gender Nonconformity and Homosexual Childhood*, edited by Matthew Rottnek. New York: New York University Press (1999).

3. Harville Hendrix, Ph.D., *Keeping the Love You Find: A Guide for Singles* (reprint edition). New York: Owl Books (2001).

4. Patrick Carnes, *Sexual Anorexia.* Center City, MN: Hazelden Publishing (1997).

5. Vivienne Cass, "Homosexual Identity Formation: A Theoretical Model," in *Journal of Homosexuality*, Vol. 4 (3), 1979.

Chapter 3
Resolve Issues With Your Family

A MAN CAN'T MAKE A PLACE FOR HIMSELF IN THE SUN IF HE
KEEPS TAKING REFUGE UNDER THE FAMILY TREE.
—Helen Keller

Of all the relationships in your life, family ties are usually the most intense and tightly organized. Most people want to stay connected to their families. There's comfort there, a feeling of safety, with people you've known virtually forever. They usually command the strongest loyalties.

But all too often, once you tell them you're gay, suddenly you're an outsider in your own family. Imagine your fear of introducing something so unexpected, perhaps so despised, that you might lose their support and respect. The prospect is chilling.

At age 42, Paul was a successful radiologist. Attractive and friendly, he came for help in coming out. He didn't want to threaten his "close-knit" family by disclosing that he was gay. In our work together, he was able to see that he'd been closeted for so long to avoid revealing his secret to potentially hostile family members. He hadn't befriended or dated gay men or entered the gay community in any way. What if a friend or relative recognized him and outed him to his family? He dreamed of moving out of state to make it easier to come out and avoid "burdening" his family.

He began to recognize that by not telling them, he'd sacrificed a lot. Because he had distanced himself, so as not to be "discovered," his family relationships had become superficial. He worried that if his sister learned he was gay she'd forbid him contact with his young nephews, whom he adored.

Paul had deep, repressed resentments toward his family. He thought they knew he was gay. "It would be so much easier if they would just ask. Then I could simply answer, 'Yes.'"

We talked about his need to take the necessary steps. Whether they suspected Paul was gay wasn't the issue. He had to take the lead.

Our work together focused on his getting the courage and finding the words to tell them. Only after doing so would it be possible for Paul to move on with his life. And as his therapy progressed, he knew this more and more surely.

When he finally did tell them, his mother and siblings were relieved. They'd all suspected but dared not ask for fear that he wasn't ready to talk. They'd trusted that he'd tell them when he was ready. Relieved, Paul could now begin to move on with his life, enter the gay community, and not worry that he would run into anyone who would tell on him.

Yes, an openly gay man risks being rejected by his family. But paradoxically, *not* talking leads the gay man to reject his family. Gays and lesbians usually *want* to tell their families but, understandably, they are scared. The very act of telling demonstrates their strong commitment to staying connected.

At age 18, I told my parents I was gay—one of the most frightening things I've ever done. I had no role models, nobody to tell me how to proceed. At that time, all the therapists and psychological literature claimed that boys became gay because of how they were raised. It was all my parents' fault! When I told them, I feared I might lose everything.

Earlier, at age 15, I'd tried to tell my mother. I was on the expressway with my driver's permit; she was in the passenger seat. It was a bright and joyous time: the Hanukkah season. But my timing wasn't ideal, and my presentation was even worse.

I started to weep, saying I had "something awful to tell her" and trying to explain how I was "different." I couldn't go on. She touched my shoulder and told me that everything would be fine. Later, she placed me in therapy.

The first therapist called my gayness a "pathology." In his words, "You were meant to be heterosexual, as everyone is. But based on how you were raised, your sexuality has become distorted. I think you could go either way, and heterosexuality is the more normative, easier route." At least he provided me with a forum to talk about my homosexuality. When I finally came out to my family, I needed that therapist to create a safe environment where I could talk about being gay. He had me describe at length my homosexual feelings, fantasies, and dreams. I became increasingly comfortable talking about my homosexuality.

I needed that, but I needed more—most obviously, I needed to be applauded for the courage to talk about myself. Straight teens receive that applause whenever they have a heart-to-heart with Mom or Dad. I needed him to affirm how much strength it took to be honest about something so difficult. I needed confirmation of the wisdom of my choice to be open about who I was. And I needed to explore myself and my sexuality without anyone telling me that straight was the better way to go.

In her article "Lesbians, Gay Men, and Their Families: Common Clinical Issues," Laura S. Brown talks about what happens when gays and lesbians do *not* tell.[1] There are three typical patterns they follow in order to avoid their families' rejection or abandonment. One is to maintain rigid emotional—and often geographical—distance from the family. They may run away from home for a life on the streets—particularly in their teen years, when they're young enough to get involved in hustling. They may simply move to another state, keeping their gayness away from the family and visiting very rarely.

The second is the "I know you know" pattern. Today, we'd call it "Don't ask, don't tell." Says Brown, "The gay person relates to his family, but with the unspoken agreement that no one will talk about the gay person's personal life." Everyone knows that "my friend" is more than a friend, but no one dares say so.

The third scenario: "But don't tell your father." The gay son is officially out to one parent or sibling, who responds with support but with a warning not to tell certain family members. Before gay children can reveal something so deep about themselves, their families must first establish an atmosphere of affection, openness, and safety.

When a son comes out of the closet, the family usually goes in. For them to say, "Our child is gay" is just as high an emotional hurdle as the one the son faced before coming out to them. Just as gay men pass through stages of coming out, so do their families. The stages are very similar.

As a psychotherapist, I've had the luxury of meeting many different kinds of men and women. I've treated many heterosexual men with the same background and childhood as mine, yet they have nary a gay bone in their bodies. How you were raised has little or nothing to do with your sexual and romantic orientation.

My parents needed to know that their son took such a big risk to tell them he was gay because he deeply valued the parent-child relationship. My parents needed to know *they* did not make me gay, that the news that I was gay couldn't "kill" anyone, and that it wasn't contagious! (I recall relatives actually warning me that if I told certain people it might kill them, or "They may decide to be gay themselves.")

Families need accurate information about homosexuality, not ignorance and misinformation. My family needed to know about those adolescent suicides linked to sexuality issues. They needed to hear that it was perfectly OK for them to disagree with me about my gayness—and to talk to me about it openly.

It's acceptable to have differences within a family. But when there's no communication, problems arise like a plague of locusts.

Nick, age 27, worked at his company's in-house employee newsletter. He was a well-adjusted young man with a promising future as a layout artist. Some years before, he had told his family—Southern Methodists who attended church regularly—that he was gay.

Nick's father wasn't at all accepting: "I didn't raise you to be a faggot. If you live in sin, I want nothing to do with you!" (I've actually heard parents tell me that they would have preferred that their child be a murderer than gay or lesbian!)

For many years since his father told him this, Nick had kept quiet about his gayness. Now, however, he had grown tired of the silence and entered therapy with me to put to rest his overwhelming feelings of sadness and grief over his father's rejection.

He decided he needed to talk, even it if meant being disowned for good. He'd come to realize that his silence was causing him much distress and that he needed to put the issue to rest by making a move himself.

And talk he did! He made several attempts to speak to his father, but his father would have none of it. Finally he looked Nick in the eye and said, "I no longer have a son," and slammed the front door in Nick's face.

Nick was devastated. During an emergency phone call soon after, he sobbed, cried, and told me what had happened. Not long afterward, he went to court and legally changed his last name to cut all ties to his father and his family.

Today, Nick has found peace within himself. He has no regrets and, more than anything, he feels sorrow for his father.

In most families the existing dynamics become exaggerated when a son comes out. Telling your family you are gay plunges them into a temporary crisis. When in crisis, people revert to old, familiar behaviors—dysfunctional or not.

If the family is religious, for example, they might become more devout. If there's alcoholism, there might be even more drinking. If family relations were strained before, they become even more distant. Family members tend to blame it all on their gay son. Worse, the gay man tends to believe he is somehow responsible for his family's adverse reaction and dysfunction.

Some healthy families address difficult issues with open discussions and sensitivity. In that case, any controversial issue—such as telling them you're gay—will be easier to deal with. Many different truths can exist in these families without anyone feeling threatened.

A kind of group energy forms in families too. Each family member is affected by your coming out, but also by other members' reactions. Family members may do anything to get you to *change back* to who you used to be so they don't have to face the truth about you or about themselves.

This "change back" syndrome becomes most obvious among the old drinking buddies of a recovering alcoholic. When the group socializes, friends might offer the man in recovery something to drink, telling him, "One won't hurt, and you're probably not an alcoholic anyway." Admitting that's a friend's in recovery can mean having to face one's own drinking problem.

When the truth is spoken, other uncomfortable and unexamined truths tend to "come out of the closet"—which makes the core issue seem even heavier than it already is. I've had clients talk about how, after they told their families they were gay, other family secrets spilled out.

Frank was a 33-year-old man referred to me following a "nervous breakdown." He had become overly anxious at his job as manager of a large hotel—which was anxiety-provoking in and of itself. As a result he was psychiatrically hospitalized for depression and anxiety.

Never married, Frank identified himself as homosexual. He stated that during his therapy in the hospital, his therapist asked why he identified himself as homosexual and not gay. Frank didn't have a good answer for that. He was out to himself, but not to anyone else locally. For a while he had lived in New York City, where he was out as a gay man to all of his friends. His job in Manhattan didn't work out, so he returned home to Michigan and went back into the closet.

Frank reported coming from a loving but not demonstrative family. He'd had a turbulent relationship with his father, who died when Frank was still in his teens. Because love wasn't openly expressed, Frank thought the neglect was his fault. He had long known he was "different," and he feared that if his parents learned about this "part of him," they might reject him. So he kept to himself, pulling away from both parents. He and his father were arguing at the time of his death and never resolved the conflict. That was also Frank's "fault."

I'm always deeply concerned when clients try to take the blame for their childhood problems. It is overwhelming for a child to believe that his parents—the adults—are not handling things, so he unconsciously makes himself the culprit.

During our work together, I coached Frank to consider coming out locally, starting with his family. We talked about how his "nervous breakdown" was a result of keeping his romantic and sexual orientation a secret. Frank began to develop a more affirmative self-concept and to identify himself as gay, not homosexual.

Ultimately, he decided to tell his mother. They cried together. A very religious woman, she urged him to try various programs in their church that offered hope and promised change. Frank told her he didn't want to change and that he was happy being gay. Then she disclosed information that was news to Frank. She said Frank's father had been a very jealous, domineering man and had competed for her attention after their five children were born. The youngest, a boy, was born with Down syndrome. Jealous of the amount of time his wife devoted to the child, the father demanded the child be put up for adoption. The mother agreed.

Frank also learned that when he was an infant, his father insisted that Frank be placed with his maternal aunt so that he and Frank's mother could both go to work. Until he was three years old, Frank lived with his aunt during the week and came home periodically.

This was very significant. Children form deep bonds with their primary caregivers in the first 18 months. Not surprisingly, Frank always felt closer to his aunt than to his own mother. Why his mother didn't take Frank home at night during the week or on weekends isn't clear, but Frank believed his pathologically jealous father was most likely glad to have his "competition" out of his home.

Coming out to his mother not only freed Frank to be more open as a gay man but also let him understand his family dynamics more fully. I assure my clients that their being gay isn't anyone's fault or responsibility. Gayness is not the result of anything anyone did or said. It is something you learn to be comfortable with, and your decision to come out lets you live your life with fewer emotional hindrances.

It's imperative that you feel good about being gay at the time you tell your family. I've found that if clients come out before they are ready, their families pick up on their ambivalence and raise doubts and difficult questions. You need to present yourself when you feel confident, assured, and certain that you are gay. If you're not fully self-actuated as a gay man and your family does engage in "change back" behavior, you might spend even more time struggling.

Again, when I told my family, I was 18 years old—and quite upset. My therapist, who was helpful in other ways, led me to believe my gayness was a consequence of having a smothering mother and a distant father. If my parents had been different, he reasoned, I would have been straight. So when I came out to my parents, I blamed them for my situation. I blamed my mother for being overprotective and told my father it was his fault I was gay because he'd left us to start a new family when I was 3.

I was angry and wanted them to feel bad. We all went screaming into family therapy—this time with a new therapist who also believed that being gay was the result of shoddy parenting. She asked, "Joe, why would you tell your family? And why did you tell them in this way?"

I was horrified and didn't answer her, because I felt shamed. She and my other therapist insisted I should change—but I couldn't, no matter how I tried. What I really needed to hear was how brave and courageous I was for telling.

The result of all this was that I went back in the closet, got a girlfriend, and lived an outward life as a heterosexual while I secretly pursued an underground gay life. Ultimately, at age 21, I found the courage to finally open that closet door, let my parents off the hook, and be responsible for my own life by presenting my gayness in a healthy way. My family was more accepting the second time around. I believe we spent more time healing from what therapy did *to* us than from my coming out.

When Will was 14 years old, his parents bought him a computer to help him with his schoolwork. Will entered gay chat rooms and began to talk to older men. Inevitably, the talk became sexual.

Susan and Tom, Will's mother and father, wondered why he was on the computer for so many hours at a time. One day they tracked the Web sites he had gone to and discovered that some were gay porn sites. They also learned he was exchanging E-mail with other gay men, some of whom were very forward sexually.

Susan and Tom were shocked. The family went to a therapist, who told them it wasn't Will who had the issue with Will's gayness, but his parents, who needed to come to terms with the fact that they had a gay son. How could a 14-year-old know his sexual and romantic orientation, they wondered. The therapist helped them see that straight and gay teenagers come to know their orientation in similar ways.

Tom and Susan went to PFLAG (Parents, Families, and Friends of Lesbians and Gays), which has numerous chapters across the country. Most of the members are straight, but many gays and lesbians attend. Within a matter of weeks, they recognized that Will was gay and accepted his gayness lovingly. They took Will to gay groups, supported his being authentically himself, and became increasingly involved in PFLAG.

Will ultimately developed a healthy self-esteem as a gay teen. He no longer talked to older men in chat rooms now that he had more appropriate outlets for his feelings. He entered college and is now a happy gay man. His parents offered him true support and didn't let their own agenda override their son's. In so doing, they gave Will a much better chance of adjusting to his gay sexual and romantic orientation than if they had decided to fight him or place their desires ahead of his.

There's a difference between privacy and secrecy. Some things are none of our parents' business and should be kept private, but being gay isn't one of them. Not telling them you are gay is secrecy, and as Alcoholics Anonymous says, "Secrets keep us sick."

Secrets also keep us feeling ashamed. To be a fully out and confident gay man means telling your parents—though not if they might injure or abuse you in some way. When violence or other life-threatening issues are at stake, then your motive becomes self-protection. In such a case it makes sense not to tell. Also, if you're dependent on them and you think they'll abandon you, then opt not to tell. Otherwise, let the differences in your family exist—risk their adverse responses. Speak *your* truth to *your* parents, whatever that truth is.

As with any family disagreement, often you'll need a "time out." If your family needs to distance themselves from you, give them their space. This is an act of love and courage on your part.

"Why did you tell us?" they might ask. "Are you trying to hurt us? Why did we need to know this?" Some of my clients' parents tell them "It's just a phase" or "If you chose that lifestyle, I just don't want to hear about it." Sometimes they just ignore the issue. "What else is new in your life?"

Many clients say that their being gay doesn't affect their parents, so they don't need to know. I disagree. Bringing over a boyfriend or a partner as "just a friend"—or not bringing him at all—means keeping secrets. That jeopardizes your relationship with everyone involved.

Usually not disclosing who you are is a result of your own reluctance to confront your family. Be truthful and say: "I choose not to tell my parents because I don't wish to face their reaction." From that place of honesty you'll grow more as a person than if you claim "They don't need to know," simply to dodge the issue.

A word of caution here. To deal with their anger, some young men take revenge against their parents. One 18-year-old who despised his mother and stepfather for making him help raise his two younger half-brothers decided to "pay them back." First, he began to advertise his gayness by his grooming. As his stepdad said, "I wish he'd stop playing with his hair." Finally, he modeled nude for a porn magazine and "somehow" contrived to have the proof photos sent to his home address for his mother to open.

When I confronted my mother for the second time, I was in Stage Five of the coming-out process—cocky and angry. She didn't want me to be gay and insisted I wasn't. This was her wish, but not the truth. Soon after I brought home two flamboyant friends who preferred to be called "Vivienne" and "Lucy." This was not a stage for them, but a way of life. In Stage Five, I needed my friends' help to release my anger at the heterosexual world and my parents. I introduced them to my mother as Vivienne and Lucy and watched her face turn white with horror.

Obviously, I don't recommend this strategy to my clients. Coming out should be free of retribution as well as guilt.

Of course, my family would have been relieved had I stayed quiet about this part of my life for good. In the movie *Torch Song Trilogy*, Arnold (Harvey Fierstein's character) fights with his mother, played by Anne Bancroft. She accuses him of pushing his sex life down her throat. He turns to her and says, "If you want to be in my life, I am *not* editing out the things you don't like." That line is very important. I show this film clip when I give talks at PFLAG and wherever families come to try to understand their children's gayness.

Murray Bowen's therapeutic work in the 1950s focused mostly on the individual. Bowen, however, noticed that he could best help an individual by looking at the family as a whole unit, with each member affecting the other. He was a pioneer in what today we call family therapy. He developed the model now known as Bowen Theory to help individuals achieve and maintain their own identity in interpersonal family relationships.

Bowen noticed that in his therapy sessions, families with problems tended to be unusually reactive to one other. They seemed to be overly influenced by one another's thoughts and feelings and had usually adopted ways to avoid one another. (As we've seen, gay men often distance themselves from their families as a way to avoid coming out to them.) Bowen's idea was that this hyperreactivity arises from a failure to gain mature independence from others' feelings and thoughts. Without the freedom to think and feel as you like, fully and honestly, your status is tenuous, fragile, and too dependent on the whims of other family members.

Following his discoveries, Bowen developed two concepts that he called *fusion*—unhealthy togetherness without boundaries—and *differentiation*, the ability to take an "I" position in one's family of origin. The "I" position enables one to define one's own position in an autonomous but nonreactive way. A critical point in Bowen's theory is that differentiation isn't achieved through breaking off relationships out of reactivity. Cutoffs sometimes imply reactivity, just like fusion.[2]

Bowen concluded that family members have a right to say "yes" to what feels appropriate for them and "no" to what doesn't. He didn't believe in relationships with no boundaries. Some people, for instance, believe that "You and I are one, and I am the one," or "You and I are one, and you are the one," rather than "We are two different people, and separate, and that is OK."

In order to achieve a state of differentiation, you must remain connected to other family members. I agree with Bowen's conclusions about the importance of families staying in dialogue with one another, even when they disagree. My experience as a therapist convinces me that being open and honest with your family is a move toward stronger ties, as is allowing them their own reactions.

The only reaction that's *not* acceptable is blame directed at you. All members must be able to express their opinions honestly—but without the intent to wound or blame. Otherwise, it's *Jerry Springer* time! If wounding or blaming occurs, then self-preservation, not reactivity, prompts a cutoff. And that is appropriate.

If family members are prone to physical violence or addictive behaviors and won't remedy the problem or get help, then protect yourself. If you try working out difficult issues with your family, do they continue to disrespect you? Are they unwilling to change their behavior or take responsibility for their part in a dysfunctional relationship? Do you keep going back, only to get emotional and mental abuse each time? Cut-offs under these circumstances are not reactive or immature.

Some family members say they want to mend and heal, but they don't want to be accountable for their role in the problem—making any relationship with them unsafe. They will say things like "I am not doing it intentionally" or "You are being too sensitive," or they'll deny their role completely and say "I don't know what the problem is" even though you have told them repeatedly. Focusing on your family's behaviors more than on what they say can often indicate the truth about how they feel about you. It may just mean they cannot say it or admit it to themselves and consequently to you.

Remove yourself from the family environment to find a more secure way to deal with them. Sometimes resolving family differences means extremely limited contact or no contact at all. Making this decision in nonreactive ways is not a cutoff. This is self-preservation.

Using Bowen's model, a gay man who comes out to his family is growing, separating in a healthy way, and letting his loved ones have their emotions even as he retains his own sense of self. In doing so, he not only helps himself and his family enjoy healthier relations, but he also better prepares himself for the differences he will encounter in a relationship with a partner.

Bowen defined self-differentiation as the state when family members are together, yet separate. Self-differentiation lets parents and children maintain their own identities apart from the family as a whole. Balancing love with the need for personal space creates self-differentiation. This is what it means to set healthy limits.

If love and limits aren't balanced, then the forces of separateness and togetherness become unstable. Family members can become self-centered, cruel to one another, overly rebellious, and disrespectful. They lack interest in one another, are emotionally cut off from the family, express false emotions and thoughts, have difficulty trusting, feel rejected, and suffer low self-esteem. If togetherness outweighs the force of separateness, members can become jealous, emotionally overinvolved, punish all negative feelings, and feel rejected for being different.

Some therapists put too much emphasis on the need for separateness. One talk-show host (who should know better) advises her callers to break contact with people who don't "behave" without trying to work things out first. In a healthy family, togetherness should be in balance with separateness. In an unhealthy family, one force outweighs the other.

Meredith, a 42-year-old mother, came to see me when her 20-year-old son, Roger, told her he was gay. She was sure this wasn't so. Her husband, Roger's stepfather, wasn't interested in attending therapy, so she came to the appointment with Roger. (Roger's father had died when he was 3, and Meredith's second husband was the only father Roger ever knew.)

Meredith started out by stating that Roger "didn't know what he was" and struggled with his sexual identity. She wanted to provide some help. Roger had come out to her only two months before, and Meredith was still devastated. She confessed that Roger, her youngest, was closer to her than her other two children. She even stated that she felt closer to Roger than to her own husband.

Roger assured her that nothing had changed and that he loved her just as much as before. He said that he was *not*, in fact, struggling with his sexual identity—he knew for sure that he was gay.

Meredith took this as an affront. "Why are you trying to hurt me like this?" she asked. Over the course of several sessions, it became clear that for years Meredith's relationship with her second husband had been weak. She had given very little to the marriage and received little in return. She had devoted all of her energy to her daughter and two sons.

Rogers's brother and sister had moved to other parts of the country, which she took as personal rejections: "I never believed I couldn't see my kids every day." Yet they remained in constant contact with her and visited her four times a year. That was not enough for her, she reported. She felt alone and abandoned. Now Roger had told her he was gay and was spending less time with her. Understandably.

She would not attend PFLAG without Roger, and her husband wouldn't go. She refused to talk to another PFLAG parent.

As a therapist, I saw red flags everywhere. This family placed a tremendous overemphasis on togetherness. Meredith had centered her life on her children, who were now adults trying to achieve separateness.

I assured her that her children's departure from the nest and regular contact were signs of her good parenting. Her children felt secure enough to make lives for themselves. But Meredith insisted these were *not* positive signs. I also praised her for having raised a gay son who was willing to share his authentic self with her. This didn't calm her either, so we moved on to the real, underlying issues.

Her recent life had centered on her daughter and sons because of her "distant" marriage. Now that the nest was empty, her chilly marriage left her feeling lonely and angry.

Soon I asked Howard, Meredith's husband, to come to our next appointment. He did—reluctantly. Though he wouldn't participate in our conversations, I gave him credit for showing up.

Roger was comfortably gay. His main issue was his mother, who was troubled over "losing" her son and suffering in a marriage that needed work. I told them Roger was on his way to a healthy gay identity, and the issue was really about their need to come to terms with having a gay son and living in a marriage based on parallel lives. Howard worked long hours and was an avid fisherman. Meredith had repeatedly asked him to spend more time with her, but Howard had resisted. I concluded that if therapy were to continue, it should focus on Howard and Meredith, which sent a message to the whole family.

Roger had done a good thing by coming out to his family, speaking the truth, and prompting Howard and Meredith to examine their own relationship.

As she became more confident about herself, Meredith was no longer so emotionally needy with her children. She also developed healthier connections with other friends and relatives. She and Howard eventually resolved the issues in their marriage—all thanks to Roger's integrity and courage. Coming out is a good thing.

References

1. Laura S. Brown, "Lesbians, Gay Men, and Their Families: Common Clinical Issues," in *Journal of Gay and Lesbian Psychotherapy*, Vol. 1 (1) 1989, page 68.

2. Michael E. Kerr and Murray Bowen, *Family Evaluation: An Approach Based on Bowen Theory*. Toronto: Penguin Books, Canada (1988).

Chapter 4
Graduate From Eternal Adolescence

WOULD THE SMALL BOY YOU ONCE WERE LOOK
UP TO THE MAN YOU HAVE BECOME?
—author unknown

The title of this chapter is a good game plan for just about anyone, gay or straight.

Anne and Duane came to see me because Duane seemed unable
to be an accountable husband and a responsible father-to-be. Anne
was angry that he spent his weekends and most of his weeknights out
with his single male friends. Totally disregarding the effects of his
behavior on his wife and future child, he came and went as he
pleased. Duane stated that he usually went out after his wife was
asleep so as not to worry her. But Anne said that it disrupted her
sleep when Duane returned home at 4 A.M. She'd wonder where he'd
been, and she felt unsafe in their marriage. Duane attributed this to
her moodiness from the pregnancy.

Unable to understand Anne's feelings, much less validate them,
he thought he should be able to do as he liked and not have her "dic-
tate" his life. He wanted her to stop judging him critically—the way
his father had—and to simply accept his behavior. But when she
asked for similar care and understanding from him, he refused, saying Anne's expectations were "unrealistic."

He thought he was a good enough husband as long as he spent

"quality" time with Anne. However, the truth was that he spent most of his leisure time away from his wife and offered her little companionship at other times.

I commented that he sounded more like a boyfriend than a husband and that being a father was going to involve a lot more time at home. He angrily replied that *he* was raised that way and it hadn't affected *him* negatively. Since Anne didn't work, he thought that she should be in complete charge of the housework and raising of their future child.

Duane was incapable of empathizing with his wife and was unwilling to be accountable for his acting out. I concluded that his problem was simple: He didn't want to have to grow up and shoulder the responsibilities of a full-time husband and father. His defensiveness indicated that he wanted it both ways—as so many teenagers do. Duane didn't want any parental constraints, which is why he projected his father's "judgments" onto his wife's legitimate complaints.

But Anne adamantly wanted Duane home more, to be with her and to parent their child. That disagreement kept them in therapy for a long while, even after their little girl was born. Neither of them was interested in divorce—especially not Duane, who liked to have his cake and eat it too.

Obviously, gay men hardly hold a monopoly on perpetual adolescence. Western society idealizes youth, which makes us want to stay youthful as long as we can. Sooner or later, adult fashions imitate youthful styles. Plastic surgeons (many of whom advertise in upscale magazines) offer to keep patients looking young.

As you'll see in Chapter 7, some psychotherapists and mental-health professionals still assume that being gay or lesbian is just a stunted adolescence. They believe that gays haven't "evolved" to the "natural" state of heterosexuality, and because we're emotionally and psychologically stuck in our teens we can't mature into wholly functional adults.

There's absolutely no truth to this. But unfortunately, gay culture does sometimes discourage growing up.

A writer friend of mine jokes, "I'm in touch with my inner child, but my inner teenager's more fun at parties!" You'll recall from Chapter 2 that the Fifth Stage of coming out releases that inner teenager. A gay man finds himself dating many men and being sexual with as many as he can. He'll have a boyfriend for a day, a week, or a month—maybe three—then it's on to the next guy.

In this stage, gay men of all ages wear T-shirts that say things like I'M NOT GAY, BUT MY BOYFRIEND IS. In Gay Pride marches, you'll hear that in-your-face chant: "We're here! We're queer! Get used to it!" In one episode of *Will and Grace,* Jack—Will's best friend, who's militantly and flamboyantly gay—was disgusted to see Grace kissing her boyfriend. Retorted the boyfriend, "We're straight, we date. Get used to it!"

Between the ages of 12 and 18, teenagers must grapple with issues of intimacy and sexuality. During their psychological development, they normally date many peers, experiment with sex and mind-altering substances, and generally act out. Their friends become their new family. They begin to assert themselves, often in a moody, anti-adult way. The gay man who's coming out also goes through a period of rebellion—except that the experience has been postponed until his adult years.

Just as the teenager *should* develop his own identity—which sometime means rebelling against his family's values—the newly out gay man no longer abides by the dominant culture's expectations of him. Indeed, a gay man *has* to be rebellious to carve out a place for himself in a heterocentric world. He follows his own line of reasoning, which doesn't necessarily comport with what makes sense to others. For any adolescent, emotional and sexual intimacy is the primary goal—just as for the gay man in Stage Five of coming out.

Unfortunately, society overlooks this delayed developmental stage in gay men and, through the lens of heterosexism, sees only an adult carrying on like a teenager—being radical, sexually promiscuous, angry, and immature. The result is a sweeping generalization: "That's just how gay men are." Because these behaviors are so visible, homophobic and homonegative writers and mental-health experts have decided that this is the "gay lifestyle." They label all gay men immature and developmentally stunted and refuse to follow the transitional stage to the end of its cycle.

But like most straight men as they reach their middle 20s, gay men eventually settle down, feel more comfortable with themselves, and become less "in your face." In Stage Six of the coming-out process, a gay man integrates his beliefs and his identity with the rest of society and no longer calls so much attention to himself. He is emotionally grown up.

Most adults—particularly parents who've been unsuccessful in developing their own sexual intimacy—are uncomfortable with adolescents' apparent success in this regard. With some jealousy, they view teenagers' demonstrative, assertive sexuality as adversarial and disobedient. But through their disrespectful behavior, teens strive to separate themselves from their families and become individuals with their own values and beliefs. This can be frightening to parents who don't know where their journey will lead.

This is also the case for gays and lesbians in Stage Five. They begin to separate and individuate, and suddenly they find themselves struggling against negative energy from the heterocentric culture, just like a teenager who starts to resist the constraints his family places on him. As a young boy, I enjoyed being Jewish. But at age 8, if I didn't enjoy it I could never have told my mother, "Look, I'm not keen on Hebrew School, so I want to go to catechism and be baptized a Catholic." She would never have allowed it—and very few families would.

Until puberty, our caretakers make us comply with their expectations of us. Then, as teens, our task is to find out who we really are. This is why coming out—not just Stage Five—is so important. You can now appreciate that any man who's still in the closet is living according to Mommy and Daddy's expectations. He hasn't become his own man. But even after coming out, he often leaves other problems in the closet behind him—though they never stay there!

For gay men who fail to complete the adolescent stage, too many problems arise for me to cover in one chapter. There's sexual addiction (next chapter), which begins as any adolescent's "normal" experimental stage but can develop into sexual compulsion. If you read the Hollywood gossip columns, you know that many straight actors suffer from this disorder. Once again, this isn't a gay issue, but a "guy" issue.

Even so, straight men generally have mothers, girlfriends, and wives who help them to grow from boys into heterosexual adults. We gay men usually lack mentors and role models (see Chapter 6). Most of us experience no social pressure to force the issue and compel us to "grow up."

Duane would have stayed young and irresponsible if not for Anne's influence. Time and again in my practice, I see wives who want their men to be more involved as fathers and husbands. Traditional male culture emphasizes competition, hunting, and scoring with women—all solitary pursuits. It's no surprise that so many men, gay and straight, do a fine job in their careers, but not in their adult relationships.

I've found that lesbians are more grown-up than most gay males. Both in and out of my practice, I see more empathy, attentiveness, connection, and maturity within their relationships. We men have a lot to learn!

Girls generally mature faster than boys do. We see this even during early development: Little girls talk earlier, are romantically interested earlier than boys—and are typically attracted to older partners. It's common for a heterosexual girl to have a crush on a boy who's still hanging out with his male buddies and doesn't even know that girls exist. Not until later do boys catch up to girls' emotional maturity. Thus it makes sense that lesbians tend to be more mature than gay men, counting in "gay years." Lesbians tend to be more serious about their lives and more organized and political. Unfortunately, many lesbians go to the extreme and find it difficult to have fun or relax.

Lesbian comedian Shan Carr recounts working on an all-gay cruise ship, where two militant lesbians found themselves at the ship's bar with the comedian and a gay male friend of hers. He was eating cheddar Goldfish from a bowl, and she was munching on peanuts. He turned to Shan and said, "Isn't this funny—you're eating nuts, and I'm eating fish!"

Both laughed. The two militant lesbians screamed, "WE DO NOT TASTE LIKE FISH!"

When Shan Carr told this joke, her audience roared.

"Some lesbians," said Carr, "don't know how to just let go and have some fun about some of the gay and lesbian differences." True, but lesbians do know how to get down to serious business in their lives and relationships.

My partner and I have been on several gay cruises. I don't know why, but they usually include about 2,000 gay men and only a dozen lesbians. And the ships' crews are usually predominantly heterosexual. The captain tells us at the "meet the captain" reception that he and the crew look forward to these cruises because we gay men "have fun, spend a lot of money, and don't complain." Crew members tell me they have a great time with us gay men and look forward to attending our parties.

I agree: Gay men do have a lot of fun, but often it's unbalanced—too much fun and not enough seriousness. I do think there's a time and place for fun and sex, but endless adolescence gets in our way. Truth is, many of us gay men abandon relationships once the painful work begins. Unlike lesbians, who generally manage to channel their anger into political activity, we gay men tend to repress our anger and difficult feelings for other men. Pleasurable feelings are allowed to surface and become sexualized. Instead of dealing with our anger directly, we tend to express it through sexual promiscuity.

Our anger also may come out sideways when we're rude and critical of other gay men. In my work with gay men and in the gay community, I find that while we might not complain to heterosexual staff or business owners, we complain a lot about one another. In fact, we have a tendency to be quite mean—just as in high school. On one gay cruise, I heard men bash the cruise's gay sponsors, who were "in it for the money" and "not genuine." In the same breath the men expressed humble gratitude for the heterosexual crew's having us on "their" boat.

Are we afraid to see our peers reaching success before us? Isn't there room for all of us? As we mature, we see that any man who makes a good living by doing something for our community is just as respectable as the heterosexual who does the same thing.

I believe that, unconsciously, we gay men allow heterosexuals their traditional privileges and attack ourselves for wanting the same. This comes from our not getting respect throughout our lives and support early on. We have to claim the respect we deserve and resist the impulse to attack other gay men.

We are a *community* of men who've been physically bashed and emotionally abused for being gay. Unfortunately, just as we begin to recover from the effects of that abuse, we begin to take it out on one another. Just like teenagers, we form our own peer groups and cliques. Those who are good-looking and in shape become popular; those who aren't attractive are marginalized. On the same cruise ship, I heard another gay man making fun of an overweight guy: "He's so big he needs his own zip code." I know the target of his remark overheard him—and I'm sure the jokester meant to be heard.

Teenagers often judge one another harshly, to cover up their own pain. As they struggle to free themselves from parental domination, they join peer groups and decide who is in or out. Gay men do the same, and they can be just as mean-spirited.

Many minorities have the same tendency to attack one another. This is called lateral discrimination: The minority group internalizes the presumed superiority of the larger society and individuals in the group act out toward one another.

If a gay man is out only to his gay friends and not to the others in his life, he may not feel challenged to move ahead. Similarly, if teenagers are isolated in their peer groups and don't have adults to help them, they won't pass through the rebellious stage in healthy ways. As gay men, we lack healthy role models to challenge us to develop concern for others—a part of the growing-up process that typically occurs during adolescence. But heterosexism and homophobia teach us not to have concerns for other gays and lesbians—only for heterosexuals.

Gay teenagers learn to avoid one another and to envy their heterosexual peers because heteronormative values are instilled in all children and teenagers. Consequently, gays and lesbians receive no information about how to deal with one another romantically and socially. We're left to cultivate humane regard for one another on our own.

If he's lucky, the man (or teenager) stuck in adolescence will hear "You'll thank me for this someday" from parents, grandparents, and others who step in to identify his adolescent behavior and challenge him to move on into adulthood. While reluctant husband Duane might resent his wife's criticisms, I thought it was good for Anne to force adulthood on him. Sadly, few gay men have people to push us in the same direction. Heterosexuals who don't have an older brother or sister can watch a child star like Ron Howard or Jodie Foster successfully progress to adulthood. We seldom have the opportunity to watch a gay boy turn into a gay teen and, finally, into a healthy gay adult.

Gay men trapped in endless adolescence have a few common traits: They believe that when hard times come, someone will rescue them. They long to be cared for like they were as children. And like children, they don't want to let the carefree times go.

We need to move on with our lives and assume adult responsibilities. This is no easy task, but one that everyone, gay or straight, has to face someday. Taking the easy way out only creates more trouble later on in life—for ourselves and for others.

For their social outlets, my "adolescent" clients go exclusively to bars where most of the men are very young and want even younger men. They spend money on things they don't need. They fly to outposts like Fire Island, Provincetown, or Key West. They squander time and frequent-flyer miles chasing big, lavish, weekend circuit parties where sex and drugs are prevalent.

If they attempt to get together privately with their "bar friends," there's no connection. They prefer superficial, short-lived, long-distance relationships. As soon as things get rocky, they move onto someone else in another state, even another country. These men dress young and judge one another by their pecs, their abs, and whatever the parking valet just put in the garage. To keep their mind off the grim reaper, they use drugs and alcohol into their 30s, 40s, and 50s.

I don't justify substance abuse at any age, but a guy in his 20s can more easily recover from its effects. Otherwise, there's nothing wrong with circuit parties or enjoying the company of younger men, but sooner or later the party's over. This necessary return to grown-up reality is frequently depicted in myths and fairy tales: At midnight, the coach turns back into a pumpkin that's too small for Cinderella to ride in. Only the glass slipper—her chance for a committed partnership—still "fits" her. Alas, too many gay men are still riding in pumpkins—they're unwilling to let go of what was important to them once, back in the days when they first came out. They hold their parents and society—but not themselves—responsible for correcting abuses and righting wrongs.

Growing up demands a realistic look at the world around us. It requires that we understand and accept that things are not fair. We need to reexamine the way we were raised and how our families function now, for good or for ill.

Like I said, growing up is no easy task. All too often, taking this closer look illuminates patterns of family dysfunction that are painful to acknowledge. To avoid this pain, we hang on to our illusions. It's easier to play the victim and complain that you have no control over a world that's out to get you. It's easier to keep looking for the unconditional love you didn't get from your family and stay out of long-term relationships that demand a growing, evolving maturity. However, by choosing the easy path you miss out on so much of the richness and beauty that life has to offer.

Eddie was a successful 42-year-old attorney who made very good money. Now that his parents were divorced and his father no longer needed the big co-op apartment where he'd grown up, Eddie resented his father for not "giving" him the place. After all, hadn't his father's alcoholism ruined Eddie's childhood? And caused Eddie to delay his coming out? And made it difficult for him to stay in relationships?

With a strong sense of self-righteousness, Eddie didn't want to admit, much less examine, his own obvious capabilities as an adult. He certainly had every right to be disappointed. But his father had every right to do with the co-op whatever he liked.

Another client, Louis, often cheated on his partner. He didn't appreciate my feedback: I told him his secrecy about his flings—which made a lie of his agreement with his partner to be monogamous—showed a lack of integrity.

This lack of communication was part of a larger problem: Louis and his partner were having relationship problems, but they wouldn't talk them out. As a result, they fought constantly and had more than a few sexual difficulties. They began to harbor negative feelings toward each other, and their sex life suffered even more. Louis insisted he had the right to go "meet other men who can meet my sexual needs, if he can't." If he discussed his problems openly and directly, his partner might tell him to leave. To avoid the risk and pain of conflict, Louis lived a double life and refused to be accountable to himself or his relationship.

What did these two clients have in common? As children, neither had his needs met. As a result, both continued to try to get adults to meet those needs—but in negative, acting-out ways. Some clients like Eddie keep going back to a parent who's unable or unwilling to give love and acceptance. When their efforts are thwarted (as they inevitably are), they usually turn to another authority figure—a boss, partner, sibling, or friend—and project their childhood problems onto this person. Of course, they expect this "surrogate" parent to supply whatever their real parents didn't give them. But the problem can never be fixed this way.

The child you once were can't get his needs met in the present. Childhood's over—it's a done deal. Trying to get someone in the present to fulfill needs unmet in the past is not just inappropriate, but it's also impossible—a sure recipe for frustration and disappointment.

Once when I was visiting my sister, I found it very difficult to understand what my 2-year-old nephew was trying to say. "He wants a drink of water," my sister explained. I had no idea how she'd made sense of his word-sounds, but she was just paying close attention, the way a mother should. Only in your early childhood can you expect others to listen to you that closely and to anticipate your needs and fight your battles for you. Now that you're an adult, it's not appropriate or realistic to expect anybody else to know what you want—you must speak up and ask for it. But even if you've built a good argument that makes sense, you might not get what you're asking for. Children are allowed temper tantrums; adults are not.

In his efforts to meet one of his childhood needs Eddie kept bumping up against the same wall: His father was still not interested in pleasing him. The same was true for Louis, who would rather go behind his partner's back than face the consequences of his own actions and choices. I wasn't surprised to learn that as a child he stole what his parents weren't willing to give him.

Neither of these men could grow past adolescence until each felt the necessary pain of recognizing that his childhood needs weren't met and never would be. As an adult, each man needed to accept responsibility for taking care of himself. The other adults in their lives had plenty to handle on their own!

David, a divorced 43-year-old gay man with a grown daughter, sought treatment to help cope with his depression. He was now in Stage 6 of coming out, and he had integrated with the mainstream culture. Several years before, he had gone through a very difficult divorce. Brenda, his ex-wife, had presented him as a villain for leaving her after a 20-year marriage. In an effort to compensate for what he saw as his wrongdoing—heterosexually marrying and then coming out of the closet—he offered her more money than even the court felt was appropriate. Although he made a decent amount of money from his dental practice, he found himself without enough money to meet his own needs.

When we explored his background, it came out that Peggy, his narcissistic mother, had run the family. To her, how things appeared to others was more important than how things actually were. She had taught her son that to get her love, he needed to please her and be her caretaker. David's father, largely uninvolved, acquiesced to whatever Peggy demanded.

David never managed to please her. He wanted to become an architect, but she told him he'd never make good money and that he should become a dentist instead. David didn't like dentistry school. But when he went to his father for direction about changing career goals, his father said, "I won't pay for your education unless you become a dentist."

At the age of 22, David felt he had no other choice but to comply with other people's expectations. When he became an adult, this script stayed with him. He married Brenda knowing he was gay. After 10 years of unhappy marriage he began to contemplate divorce, only to hear negative judgments from both his mother and wife: "How would it look for a man with a little child to divorce?" He stayed married to a wife who berated him constantly, called him names, told him he wasn't a good father, accused him of hiding money, and constantly demanded to know his whereabouts.

David felt his gayness acutely. He buried it under alcohol abuse and took appointments on weekends to avoid going home. But he eventually received a wake-up call: Prostate cancer forced David to assess his life. He decided to stop using alcohol and enter a 12 Step program. During his early recovery, he began to face some of the problems he'd avoided before. Now that his daughter was grown, he became increasingly intolerant of his wife's emotional abuse. His urge to come out of the closet grew stronger now that he no longer anesthetized his feelings with alcohol. Still, his situation caused him a great deal of anxiety. How could he let down his wife—and his parents, of course!—by not only coming out but also by reducing the family income? After their divorce, Brenda would have to take a job, and his daughter would have to fend for herself financially. How would that look to others?

Through therapy, David discovered that his childhood family script still ruled his life. He'd never grown up—or more accurately, he had never outgrown the shame-induced docility that had been drummed into him as a boy. Looking back, he'd tried his best to follow the privileged heterosexual model to the letter: Get a lucrative education, get married, and make good money to support his family. The only problem was he never wanted this scenario. He wanted to come out, find a satisfying relationship, and become an architect. But because of how those choices would have "looked," he elected to please everyone except himself. The tragedy, of course, was that he'd failed at that too!

Now David was living on antidepressant medication. His only way out was to challenge his family script and, while it wasn't an easy task, to learn that it was OK not to please others. He needed to confront his wife's, daughter's, and parents' judgments and not let them rule his life.

After many long months of therapy, David divorced Brenda. Even though he'd covered all his daughter's college expenses, she stopped talking to him because he stopped paying her car installments and credit card bills. He simply couldn't afford it. In addition, he had to admit that he'd given his child too much all along to compensate for the loving support he'd never gotten from his own parents.

Next, David had to face an even harder challenge—confronting the family messages he'd received while growing up. His first response to my suggestion was, "I feel you're encouraging me to bash my parents." I wasn't, of course. Instead, I was inviting him to examine—for himself and on his own—his negative feelings about how he was raised. I wanted him to see how burying those feelings shaped his current life.

His mother and father, who strongly opposed his divorce, continued a relationship with Brenda. There was nothing wrong with their wish to see the mother of their granddaughter, but it *was* wrong for Brenda to continue to berate David and to put him down in front of their daughter. (Georgia's Cobb County has established a practice that I wish more communities would adopt. Parents planning to divorce are required to take a class on how to treat their children. The course emphasizes that neither parent should ever disparage or put down the absent parent in front of the kids.)

Of course, David's parents telephoned him to describe the pain Brenda was going through. How could he inflict all this pain on her, they wondered, just to have sex with men? David needed to confront his parents—at the ripe old age of 43! He initially told them, "Stop interfering in my life." Not listening, they replied, "This is our life too, and Brenda is the mother of our grandchild."

Clearly, nothing David said or did would ever satisfy them. On top of everything else, they were angry because Brenda's mother snubbed them at church. In their view, this was all *David's* fault—fallout from his divorce. With my help, he decided to tell his parents that if they insisted on talking about Brenda or his former in-laws, he'd stop the conversation and hang up. They continued; he hung up. Over time, they stopped. But for David, the process of learning to hold his ground was very difficult. He had to recognize that his parents weren't looking out for *his* best interests, but for their own. Their only concern was how his actions made them look in the eyes of their social associates. Now it was time for David to make *himself* feel good—and let his parents feel their *own* pain over his newfound independence.

Remember, we all have two sets of parents: the ones who raised us and the internalized ones inside of us. We have to confront what Freud called the superego, along with all the scripts we've followed since childhood. What fits now, and what doesn't? Abandoning scripts that no longer fit can be surprisingly painful. Are you disobeying and disrespecting what your parents want for you? Yes—moving away from adolescence requires that you disappoint others. Separation and individuation is what adulthood is all about. It's not disrespectful to honor your *own* journey. However, if your family threatens to reject you, it makes growth to adulthood vastly more challenging. This is just as true when you are coming out as when you're "out" on your own.

In graduating from endless adolescence, a son feels *separation guilt* over individuating from his family. Quite often, his family has given him subtle or overt messages that his separation will injure them. There are many jokes about the Jewish mother who states, "If you really loved me, you wouldn't leave me," but I don't think they're funny. I've seen the negative effects this kind of clinging has on clients trying to make an adult life for themselves.

Separation guilt is particularly common among clients who are conflict-avoidant. Usually, they also have trouble living as openly gay men. And because they won't be more fully out, their partners often get frustrated or leave. They have few gay friends, because going to gay establishments causes them too much anxiety. They associate all these troubles with their belief that being gay is particularly difficult.

After some time in therapy, it becomes apparent that most of these men were raised in families where the message was, "Don't talk about your feelings, do as we say, and don't make waves." Being gay goes against a conflict-avoider's life script. Indeed he'll do anything to avoid conflict—even if it means destroying his life. But a gay man *must* make waves in a society that wants gays to be quiet and that condemns people who live outside the norm.

At age 38, Josh had been partnered with a man for two years. He reported he didn't feel much of anything about his relationship, about being gay, or about anything else in life. He had begun to come out several years before I met him, but he'd never felt good about his homosexuality. He wasn't attracted to women, romantically or sexually, which troubled him greatly.

He attributed this to homophobia and heterosexism, but there was more to his story. Josh's alcoholic father had abused his wife and kids verbally and physically. Many times Josh listened to his father's rages after a night of drinking and came downstairs to find the living room turned upside down. One time after his father beat her, his mother was taken to the hospital.

Josh's father saw anything that went against his demands as a threat. If Josh talked back, his father either intimidated him or beat him. Early on, Josh learned not to cause waves that could precipitate violence. During his teenage years, he never rebelled. Nor did he establish a separate sense of self.

When Josh was 14, his father divorced his mother and married a woman with whom he'd been having an affair and who had children of her own. Josh's father considered them his new "family." Abandoned and rejected, Josh felt he hadn't been a good enough son and had caused his father to leave.

Children often make themselves "bad" to absolve their errant parents—they blame themselves for their feelings of rejection and pain. In his 20s, Josh knew better than to come out. He knew his father would be angry and might even incite the rest of the family to reject him too. His mother hadn't protected him as a child—why would she defend him now?

Josh dated women and tried to make a go of heterosexuality. His attempts to be a "good boy" pleased his family, but not him. Then Josh joined a men's choir group, where he befriended some gay men. He liked them, became closer to them, and began to realize he was gay. But here, of course, he ran into trouble. Being gay meant going against the rules of a heterocentric society—and his family's rules as well. Now in his 30s, Josh had lived his entire life as an obedient son who always followed the rules and became angry at people who didn't.

Then he met Jack and started a relationship. But after several years together, Josh told me he still didn't feel love for his partner or comfort with his gay identity. In therapy, he recognized that as a youngster he'd made an unconscious decision to behave like the "best little boy in the world" to avoid conflict, trouble, and beatings. Even if he hadn't been gay, Josh knew he would eventually have to risk his family's disapproval to be true to his values. His fundamentalist father and stepbrother often made disparaging comments about gays and lesbians. How could Josh admit he was one of those who were "all going to hell"?

His gay life was the main arena in which he acted out these conflicts. As his relationship with Jack progressed, the sexual side of their relationship dwindled until Josh was no longer interested in sex. This occurred about three months after they met. Typically, sexual feelings diminish within the first six to 18 months after a relationship begins—Josh's rapid loss of interest was unusual. Throughout his life, Josh had viewed sex as bad and dirty; in fact, he aspired to be asexual. Why?

Josh's story is typical of gay men who seek to avoid conflict. His father's violence and his mother's passivity had taught him that disapproval meant physical abuse and rejection.

He knew he should be angry with his father but didn't feel it. Conjuring up any direct anger, he felt guilty, as if he were "bashing" the man. To protect his father, Josh had generalized his anger toward the world. In our therapy appointments, Josh often raged against the government, whose laws didn't offer protection to gays and lesbians, and talked about feeling "powerless" and "helpless." This type of anger is necessary and appropriate, but Josh's overreaction ate at him and left him anxious and depressed. He languished in an unsatisfying, low-paying job, lived a secret, closeted life, and lacked emotion and sexual passion.

For Josh, having sex with another man meant having to admit he was gay. By shutting down his sexuality on the grounds that sex was "nasty and dirty," Josh kept himself developmentally at age 14, when his father divorced his mother to marry another woman. He was psychologically stuck in that time of his life.

He couldn't feel love for his partner because he hadn't gone through the intimacy stage of development—the normal, healthy time when teenagers begin to form attachments to people outside their families. As a child, Josh had decided never to seek relationships outside his family. His dependence on them made it difficult for him to acknowledge what they'd done to him.

In individual therapy, Josh grew defensive about his family and was very protective of them. In group, he defended the parents of other group members, even as the members recounted the dysfunctional and abusive things their families had done to them. Whenever a group member had a breakthrough, Josh questioned the validity of therapy and discounted its effectiveness. "We're being brainwashed," he'd shout, even though he knew that wasn't true. He was a neutered, scared, depressed, and angry man who had let his father and mother off the hook.

Josh said, "That's the past. It's over. Let's move on." I agreed, but I also argued that he couldn't move on until he learned to allow himself to enjoy adult sexuality, an intimate relationship with a partner, and the satisfaction that comes with resolving conflicts. This was the crux of his problem. By living as an asexual underachiever, Josh successfully kept himself "bad" in order to let his parents remain "good" in his mind.

Survivor guilt arises when you achieve more than your parents did. Originally, the term was used to describe the emotions felt by those who survived the Holocaust when other loved ones or family members did not. For related reasons, adult children can find it very difficult to leave home. They know they must go on with their lives, but leaving their parents behind is profoundly disturbing. I've had clients who sabotaged their own careers lest they become more successful than their parents—which was taboo, according to the message their parents had sent them. *Why should you have things any better than I did?* My client Max came from a lower-middle-class background and rose to prominence in his marketing career. His partner was a worldly man who understood the finer things in life. One night, the two of them accompanied Max's parents to a restaurant that didn't serve alcohol but encouraged patrons to bring their own. At the liquor store, Max's mother selected an inexpensive wine she enjoyed. Max and his partner—a wine connoisseur—selected one of the imported vintages they'd grown to like.

Max's mother saw the price and asked, "Why buy something so expensive when the cheaper wine is just the same?"

Max explained why the expensive wine tasted better and that they'd learned to enjoy it.

"Well," she said, "don't forget the time when you were broke and didn't know anything. So don't think you can fool me with your wine connoisseur talk!"

Max was crushed. How could his own mother say something so insulting? I explained that this had been her way of communicating that he hadn't grown bigger or better than the rest of his family. Threatened with his newfound knowledge, she engaged in "change back" behavior (as discussed in chapter 3)—she tried to change Max back into the man he was originally. Once he understood this, her remarks no longer bothered him.

Explaining this makes it all sound simple, but I know it's not. Gay and straight alike, all children are hardwired to be loyal—to protect their parents and not to hold them accountable. It can be extremely painful to reflect on the negative, abusive things your parents have done. It's not a question of bashing or blaming, but of identifying facts. It's not about making your parents right or wrong, good or bad—everyone's a little of both—but about looking at your real feelings about your childhood and moving forward into adulthood.

For gay men, the journey goes even further. In his autobiography, *The Best Little Boy in the World* (originally published under a pseudonym), Andrew Tobias writes about his efforts to conceal his gayness, about which he was most ashamed. In addition, the "best little boy" dared not speak a negative word about his parents, lest he be abandoned, rejected, or physically harmed.

The way out of adolescence is to confront our childhood messages and challenge their validity in our lives today. Does that mean addressing the issues with your parents or childhood caretakers directly? Possibly. It definitely means confronting your internalized parents and caretakers—the ones who live inside of you, as you'll see in Chapter 7. But it can also be healing and helpful to sit down with your parents and "kick around" things you remember from childhood. It's important for your inner gay child to see that he's not little any longer, and that his parents aren't superhuman, but just people, like he is.

For most people this is dangerous territory. Like Josh, many clients believe I'm advising them to be hateful to their parents. I hear questions like, "My parents are old now. What's the point?" or, "They're so good to me now. Why bring up all the hurtful things they did in the past?" In sessions with me, clients often find that simply talking about their parents—simply reviewing the facts and feeling the pain attached to those facts—makes them feel guilty. The facts make it impossible for them to deny their parents' negative behavior. Inevitably, negative feelings follow.

In addition they get in touch with their grief—about what their parents did not do for them and were unable to give them in childhood. In her best-selling book, *The Drama of the Gifted Child,* Alice Miller addresses how children adapt to their parents' needs in order to please them, even at a very early age.[1] In doing so, children lose their true identity and authentic selves. They learn not to feel their most intense feelings, knowing these feelings are considered undesirable by their parents. Miller believes, as do I, that once this grief and pain are addressed, in adulthood, a "new authority" over one's self emerges. Until people recognize and accept what they did and didn't get from their childhood, they cannot move forward in their therapy. Nor can they enter adulthood in a full, satisfying way.

Fifty-year-old Geoff came to me because he couldn't find a relationship. He claimed to be out, said he felt good about being gay—but confessed he was mainly attracted to straight men. He'd even gone so far as to invite his straight friend Jim to be his roommate in his two-bedroom apartment.

Jim knew Geoff was gay and made it clear he was straight—which only excited Geoff more. Geoff made it clear he was interested in sex, but Jim politely declined, saying he was "not that way."

Geoff asked to watch while Jim worked out in his bedroom. Jim, feeling that wouldn't be too threatening, agreed. Then Geoff asked to masturbate while watching. Again Jim agreed, as long as he didn't have to see it. Eventually, Jim allowed Geoff to fellate him while Jim watched heterosexual porn videos. Jim wasn't the least bit interested in Geoff's body or in any sexual—or affectionate—reciprocation. He was having his own trouble with women and found it flattering to have Geoff "worshiping" him.

Some people might label Jim as a closeted gay or bisexual. I don't agree. Plenty of straight men are willing to let another man pleasure them, especially if they can arouse themselves with heterosexual imagery—or even have women in the room. A man's sexual *behavior* doesn't necessarily reflect his preference or orientation. As you'll see in the next chapter, sex addicts often feel driven to take whatever satisfaction they can, wherever they can.

Geoff was troubled because he wanted an emotional relationship with Jim, which wasn't feasible because Jim wasn't even bisexual. In therapy with me, Geoff admitted that his fascination with straight men in general, and Jim in particular, kept him from feeling better about being gay and finding a long-term partner.

Geoff worried whenever Jim stayed out late with friends of his own. Geoff asked Jim to call him and repeated that he had feelings for him. Predictably, Jim was bothered by Geoff's insistent romantic interest and threatened to cut off their sexual relationship if Geoff didn't stop pursuing him emotionally. This caused Geoff tremendous grief.

I have a close friend, Alan Semonian, who tells people, "I'm bi and can go either way. I like gay men, and I like straight men!" Some pornographic films and stories feature a gay man seducing a straight man. On the Internet, many gays cruise specifically for married men (who are, presumably, straight). But why should a gay man desire straight men and want to pursue them?

In *Arousal: The Secret Logic of Sexual Fantasies,* Michael J. Bader discusses a similar dynamic—heterosexual women who are attracted to gay men and "may become sexually expressive with such men in a more confidant and spontaneous way than they can with straight men."

"The issue here is clearly one of safety. Gay men make it safe for these women to become sexually aggressive, because the women know that their overtures won't be reciprocated. [They] have anxieties about being sexual with straight men because they're afraid of being overpowered or rejected, on the one hand, or of hurting the man with their sexual power, on the other. In either case, the fact that the gay man won't cross the line between playful flirting and real sexual behavior is intensely reassuring to such women."[2]

Many people believe that gays are attracted to *all* members of their own sex. This argument is used to keep gays out of the military. But just as a straight man isn't attracted to every woman, a gay man isn't attracted to every man. Moreover, even if a gay man is attracted to a straight man, he won't necessarily act on his attraction. But that's precisely what many heterosexual men are afraid of—being objectified and reduced to a sexual object. If a straight man has been a sexual aggressor in his pursuit of women, why shouldn't gay men treat him the same way? In projecting his own guilt, he wrongly assumes all gay men want to ogle him in the showers or at urinals.

The gay man who lacks boundaries around straights or has unresolved sexual feelings often realizes—consciously or not—that because his overtures won't be reciprocated, it's "safe" to flirt with straight men and fully release his sexual energy. (Of course, it's not safe for gay men to express their sexual interests directly, because straight men can get offended and react violently.)

Was Geoff avoiding sex—and thus intimacy—with gay men? He knew that to some degree he was, but his awareness was more cognitive and "rational" than emotional. Again and again, clients tell me they grasp the dynamics of their situation, but their understanding is totally intellectual, "above the neck." They don't feel these insights at a gut level, which is what therapy often helps them to achieve.

In short, Geoff could have sex with Jim while avoiding *emotional* intimacy. Geoff received nothing but the sight of a hunky straight man lifting weights, and a penis to service every now and then. Beyond that, there was no touching, no affection, nothing in return.

There's a well-known, obvious parallel among young girls who develop obsessive crushes on a rock star or "teen heartthrob" who's utterly unobtainable. The girls find a "safe" object for their blossoming sexuality. In similar fashion, gay men who focus on straights keep intimacy at bay, confident that any sexual relationship will remain superficial. But this isn't healthy. Adult sexuality must evolve. These men—like teenage girls—postpone their relational development by nipping emotional involvement in the bud.

If you've ever entertained the fantasy of helping a closeted man discover his real preference, welcome to the club! Straight men (and countless female readers of so-called "bodice-ripping" romances) relish the scenario of the virile male as sexual mentor—breaking down a woman's inhibitions and initiating her into full-fledged adult sexuality.

Many gay men enjoy the company of their straight coworkers and friends. But if a gay man prefers "converting" straight men over seeking intimacy with another gay man, there's a problem.

Very often arrested adolescence means that a man puts his emotional development on hold, pending an ongoing search for acceptance from—and connection to—his father. His father was straight, so he longs for the affection of straight men like his father.

This also helps explain the appeal of the fantasy of the straight man who, ultimately, begins to enjoy gay sex. He doesn't just *like* his gay sexual partner, he *approves* of him. And, by his behavior, he admits that his previous homophobia was wrong. This kind of wish fulfillment is usual for the gay man working through an unresolved relationship with his primary role model: his father.

Face it, what other straight man had such a big impact on your life? Here, the gay man "wins over" his father-surrogate through his sexuality—which, of course, was the source of contention in their relationship. If problems with one's father are not resolved, it's impossible to grow up and leave childhood behind.

In Internet chat rooms, you'll see another very common fantasy: the heterosexual man who wants to sleep with another man's wife while the husband watches. Freud wrote about the Oedipal complex, wherein the 3-year-old wants to kill off Daddy and have Mommy all to himself. The adulterer's kick isn't sex, but domination: The woman's husband is the "humiliated loser." Symbolically, a little boy "wins" his Mommy and makes Daddy watch.

Please understand, I'm not condoning incest! But many studies indicate that children identify with the parent of their same sex. Boys pattern their behavior after their fathers—often unconsciously. A straight male client confessed to me, "I left my wife for a married woman. My father let us move in with him. Only later did I realize this behavior ran in the family. Long after my girlfriend and I broke up, my Dad kept up his 21-year affair with a married woman."

Nowhere do I see this more clearly than at my weekend workshops for gay men, where I explore the "father wound." This is usually a turning point in the workshops—so much unfinished business with fathers needs to be explored and healed—for all men, gay and straight alike. In the men's movement literature, there are plenty of books that address men's relationships with their fathers. For gay men, however, most books and writings discuss how fathers influence their sons' homosexuality. I don't agree that any particular type of relationship with a father contributes to a homosexual orientation, but I do believe that gay sons have different types of issues with their fathers than heterosexual sons.

For the most part, heterosexual sons experience emotional distance from their fathers because their fathers work long hours, drink, or divorce their wives. But straight fathers and sons share a heterosexual orientation—the sons can bond with them or other heterosexual father figures. Gay men don't have this advantage.

At my weekend workshops and therapy groups, I coach gay men to get closer to their father wounds. The room always quiets, breathing becomes shallow, and tears fill many eyes. Getting closer to their fathers either physically or just in their minds is a profound experience. For some, this is so difficult they either pass on the whole exercise at the workshop or, in group, avoid the discussion altogether.

Another issue is that gay men often feel inferior to straights. When I started my gay men's groups, participants needed to understand that we were a group of men who happened to be gay. The word *men* was very significant, and as gay *men* we had to claim our masculinity.

I encourage gay men to go to their fathers and propose that the two of them heal and grow together. Most of my clients and workshop participants say they're uncomfortable going to their fathers, either because their fathers are elderly or because they won't listen. The issue usually isn't whether the father will be able to handle the confrontation. In any case, it's important that gay men return to the original source of their masculinity, regardless of the prospects for a successful resolution to any problems.

Of course, I don't recommend confrontation if one's father is abusive, violent, or dangerous in any way. Otherwise, I see a *lot* of good work to be done here. In the men's movement, Robert Bly and John Lee are just two of the many activists who encourage men to go to their fathers. We gay men should follow their lead.

References

1. Alice Miller, *Drama of the Gifted Child: The Search for the True Self.* New York: Basic Books (1981).

2. Michael J. Bader, Ph.D., *Arousal: The Secret Logic of Sexual Fantasies.* New York: St. Martin's Press (2002).

Chapter 5
Avoid (or Overcome) Sexual Addiction

PLEASURES MAY COME OUT OF ILLUSION, BUT HAPPINESS
CAN ONLY COME OUT OF REALITY.
—Nicholas Chamfort

In 1997, Patrick Carnes and Robert Weiss developed the Gay and Bi-Sexual Addiction Screening Test (G-SAST) to help assess sexually compulsive or "addictive" behaviors. To take this adaptation of the test, simply give yourself one point for every Yes answer. A score of 13 or higher may indicate issues that you need to explore.

1. Was I sexually abused as a child or teenager?
2. Have I subscribed to, or regularly purchased, sexually explicit magazines?
3. Do I regularly rent or buy sexually explicit videos?
4. Did my parents have trouble with their own sexual or romantic behavior? (For example, did they have extramarital affairs or flirt with other family members?)
5. Do I find myself preoccupied with sexual thoughts or planning sexual encounters?
6. If I enjoy phone sex lines and online porn Web sites, has my use of them ever exceeded my ability to pay for these services?
7. Do significant others, friends, or family ever worry aloud or complain about my sexual behavior—as opposed to my sexual orientation?

8. I have trouble stopping patterns of sexual behavior even when I know they're dangerous to my health.

9. I spend time viewing pornography, enjoying phone sex, and logging onto cybersex chat rooms. Does that outweigh the time I spend in intimate, face-to-face "live" contacts with romantic partners?

10. When talking frankly and honestly with my friends and/or partners, do I hide or minimize the extent or nature of my sexual activities?

11. I can't wait for social events with friends or family to be over with so that I can go out and get some action.

12. Are bathhouses, sex clubs, and/or video arcades a regular—or preferred—part of my sexual activity?

13. Do I think or worry that anonymous or casual sex has kept me from achieving long-term intimate relationships—or other personal and creative goals?

14. Once the sexual "novelty" of a new partner has worn off, do I have trouble maintaining an intimate relationship?

15. Have I ever cruised public rest rooms, rest areas, and/or parks to look for sexual encounters with total strangers?

16. Do my sexual hook-ups place me in danger of arrest—for lewd conduct or public indecency?

17. Have I ever been approached, warned, charged, and/or arrested by police or private "rent-a-cop" security personnel for engaging in sexual activity in a public place?

18. Do I have reason to worry about contracting HIV and other STDs but still keep engaging in risky, unsafe sexual behavior?

19. Has any partner or friend of mine ever been hurt emotionally as a result of my sexual behavior (again, *not* my sexual orientation)? Have I ever found it simpler and easier to lie to someone I care about? Have I shown up late for a family reunion, wedding, or business appointment because a sexual liaison slowed me down?

20. Does sex help me forget or escape my problems and anxieties?

21. After having sex, do I ever feel troubled, guilty, or ashamed?

22. Have I made myself promises to change some form of my sexual activity—only to break them later, again and again?

23. Does my sexual activity (again, *not* my sexual orientation) interfere with professional or personal goals I've set for myself? After a late night of sexual activity, can I still do my best at my career? Has it damaged or ruined any relationship of value—friendship, romantic, or family?
24. Have I ever paid for sex? (Not necessarily in cash!)
25. Have I ever had sex with someone just because I was feeling horny and aroused at the time—but later felt ashamed or regretful, wishing that encounter never took place?

In the gay community, sexual addiction is a touchy subject that's rarely discussed. While all men—gay, bi, and straight alike— can suffer from this disorder, gay men tend to see any criticism of their sexual behavior as yet another attempt to pathologize their sexuality as a whole and to judge it by heterosexual standards.

I understand that concern, but it's also vital to recognize that lives can be ruined as a result of excessive sexual behavior. My own working definition of "addiction" is any activity that interferes in your life in some way, but that you continue, despite the negative consequences.

Patrick Carnes has written extensively on the subject. In fact, he coined the term in the subtitle of his landmark book, *Out of the Shadows: Understanding Sexual Addiction,*[1] which helped a great many men identify behaviors that caused them distress. Carnes's book didn't address gay men in particular, but his more recent book, *Don't Call It Love: Recovery From Sexual Addiction,* includes examples of gay men and their sexual behaviors. He lists a number of signs of sexual addiction. One is *a pattern of sexual behavior that's out of control.* Of course, sexual impulses are the spice of life, reminding us that we're biological beings! But in sexual addiction, these feelings become intrusive. An impulse is followed by a strong need to act on that urge *immediately,* to get relief. When this pattern begins to occur with some regularity, the sufferer can begin to track it.

Severe consequences due to one's sexual behavior constitute another warning sign. These consequences may include being arrested, compulsive masturbation, contracting sexually transmitted diseases, having a loving relationship end when your partner catches you cheating, or actual bodily harm. I have nothing against those who wish to play in S&M scenes. However, people in the scene will tell you rules exist: Trust—which means establishing a "safe word" at the start—is a top priority. But a sex addict tends to bypass safeguards because he finds thrill in the risk. Danger is totally disregarded for the sake of the high.

Eli Coleman, who is affiliated with the human sexuality program at the University of Minnesota Medical School, has written extensively on sexually compulsive behavior.[2] He believes that "addiction" isn't an accurate description for this disorder. He believes what he calls sexual compulsivity is "driven by anxiety-reduction mechanisms, rather than by sexual desire."

John Money, a pioneering sexologist and author, refers to "lovemaps" that were created in your childhood by your caretakers and the culture you were raised in. Healthy lovemaps evolve within a community that encourages affectionate caregiving and recognizes sex as natural and attaches no taboo or stigma to the sex act. Money sees sexually compulsive behavior as the result of a lovemap that's been "vandalized" through physical, emotional, and sexual abuse.[3]

I've found these three pioneering models to be effective in my work with sexually compulsive gay men. The best approach may be different for different clients, though some clients benefit from a mixture of all three. For one person, the addiction model may suggest a behavioral and cognitive path to recovery. For another whose behavior is an anxiety-reducing form of obsessive-compulsive disorder (OCD), medication can help. Finally, viewing the behavior as a vandalized lovemap may spur inquiry into a client's childhood and early abuse: "Who were your caretakers? How did you develop your concepts of love and intimacy?"

Another factor that contributes to sexual addiction is the homophobic claim that being gay is just a matter of sex and nothing more. Over time, many gay men begin to believe this and thereby become prime candidates for sexual addiction. I call this "covert cultural sexual abuse." I believe gay men especially suffer from this form of abuse.

Overt sexual abuse involves direct contact, such as fondling and penetration. Covert abuse involves indirect contact such as a lecherous stare, sexual language, and inappropriate hugs or kisses. Here, the victimized people walk away from the encounter feeling "icky" but can't put their finger on why. Similarly, I believe that exposure to media reports about hate crimes, antigay legislation, and religious epithets are a form of emotional and psychological abuse, albeit on a covert level. This very strong negative impact can be a strong influence on gay men and can contribute to sexual addiction.

About covert sexual abuse: When I ask clients, "Were you ever sexually abused?" they say "No, of course not." But after I educate them on the covert forms, their answers often change.

When a gay man comes out, covert abuse intensifies. People call him—behind his back, usually—"faggot," "pole-smoker," or "cocksucker," among other epithets. Of course, this is also an attempt to control him by discouraging his sexual behavior and alienating him from whatever group he's part of. This is covert cultural abuse, it vandalizes our lovemaps, and it's a strong contributor to sexual addiction.

Obviously, there's no consensus on the definition or the method of assessing sexual addiction and compulsion. For simplicity's sake, I'll use "sex addict" to refer to any gay man wrestling with this issue. As the earlier questionnaire suggests, if you've tried to stop or cut down on cruising behavior with no success, that's a warning sign. Addictive behavior often displays a progressive increase in tolerance. This syndrome explains heroin overdoses: Because the previous dose of the drug wasn't satisfying, the frustrated junkie "promotes" himself to a stronger dose—beyond what his body can handle.

Similarly, the sex addict requires more of whatever behavior satisfied him in the past. Because this progression occurs over time, it's not always obvious to the sufferer. Initially, masturbation with fantasy is enough to satisfy his sexual appetite. Later, he needs to view pornography while masturbating. Then he feels the need to actually meet someone. Suddenly, he's cruising at a gay bar or sex club, or going online more often than he wants to.

Ironically, this progression reflects the normal evolution of healthy sexual development: Fantasy, leading to masturbation, leading to a sexual partner is normal. Cruising gay bars or sex clubs, or going online, can be recreational fun. Some men need fantasies to achieve orgasm with their partner. These behaviors, in and of themselves, don't constitute addiction, unless they interfere with one's being completely present with one's partner and enjoying sex—*in addition* to the fantasy.

Problems crop up when, despite negative consequences, a man feels the urge to act out risky behaviors that most men could enjoy safely in their imaginations. Other sex addicts remain at the fantasy level—all they want is fantasy, which keeps them from experiencing intimacy with anyone else.

People with addictions deny or honestly don't perceive the consequences of their behavior. I used to work at a chemical dependency center, and clients often told me things like "If my spouse would just stop complaining, then my drinking wouldn't be a problem" or "If I didn't live in Michigan, then I could take mass transit and I wouldn't have all those drunk-driving convictions."

Accordingly, I responded, "Well, this is the spouse you're married to," or "You *do* live in Michigan! So as a result, you have a problem with your drinking." Only when a client becomes accountable for his own behavior and ceases to blame it on others can treatment begin.

The physical withdrawal symptoms for addictions to alcohol and drugs are fairly well known. But most people don't realize that during any addictive behavior, natural chemicals such as endorphins and adrenaline are released within the body—which makes these actions even more compelling. The sex addict's behavior causes chemical changes in his brain that promote a mood- and mind-altering experience.

Another natural drug called phenylethylamine, PEA for short, is an essential chemical for those addicted to inherently risky behaviors like gambling, shoplifting, bungee jumping, and sex. PEA's molecular structure parallels amphetamine's, and like amphetamine it's strongest when first released. (Many addicts say they're always seeking the feeling they had during their first high.)

Both PEA levels and sexual arousal are dramatically enhanced by the presence of danger. The higher the fear and risk involved, the more PEA is released. This helps explain the experience of exhibitionists, who like having sex outdoors or in a motel room with the curtains open. Part of the thrill is the danger of being caught. Unfortunately, undercover police officers, disguised as fellow cruisers, actively arrest men who loiter in rest areas and public bathrooms. The result? Handcuffs, humiliation, and a night in jail. Fines and attorney's fees in the thousands of dollars often follow.

One treatment suggestion for the sex addict in early recovery is to refrain from all sexual behaviors, even masturbation. The idea is to let him create some distance from sexual behavior and obtain a more objective perspective. Many therapists, including Patrick Carnes, advise a three- to six-month period of celibacy. But as with any other addiction, someone who stops excessive sexual behaviors can experience withdrawal symptoms, because his body is used to relying on the natural neurochemicals released during the acting-out behavior. Some of the physical symptoms that clients in the early stages of recovery frequently report to me—and reported in Carnes's hospital studies—include headaches, nausea, chills, sweats, and itchy skin, possibly because the body is no longer numbed by high doses of neurochemicals. During celibacy, psychological changes may include:

Fatigue. Because the addict no longer raids his internal pharmacy for "hits" to get him going, he may feel more tired than usual.

Anxiety and depression. If sexual addiction has been a way to manage anxiety, it may surface once the activity stops. I hear clients complain of tension, nervousness, even rapid heartbeat. Since many addicts use sexual behavior as a way to cope with stress, they may suffer periods of insomnia, irritability, "the blues," feelings of hopelessness and helplessness, and changes in appetite.

Both high and low sexual arousal. Some clients report being flooded with sexual thoughts and urges—more so than while they were sexually acting out. Others say that their libido shuts down entirely and they worry about becoming asexual.

According to the men I've treated, these symptoms usually last 14 to 15 days. For some, however, they can last 10 weeks.

Not all men can achieve celibacy, and not every man needs to observe a period of celibacy to achieve a quality recovery. Most important is to at least *work* to stop sexual practices that put one at risk—though many of my clients still experience some withdrawal symptoms just from halting their most dangerous behaviors. Instead of shaming a man's inability to achieve total celibacy, I take him from where he is and work on his strengths. This is particularly important for gay men. So many of us have been forced into "canned" heterosexual models that we resist the idea that there is only one route to any solution. In response to the ultimatum "My way or the highway," we choose the open road.

For some, the goal is to quit looking at porn, online or otherwise. This allows the gay man to date and explore, being sexual in safe ways with flesh-and-blood partners. Men who can stop their most compulsive behaviors still feel some withdrawal symptoms, though perhaps not as acutely.

When Bill entered therapy, he admitted to having a strong sex drive. He found himself engaging in sexual behavior every single day, either through masturbation or hook-ups with other men. Long-term, he wanted to explore hobbies and pursue romantic relationships, but his compulsion to act out sexually was blocking his progress. His New Year's Eve resolution was to masturbate "only" a few times a week and to view Internet porn only on Saturday nights. He tried to pare his Internet time from five hours to 60 minutes or less. The longest he could refrain from masturbation was two weeks.

There's nothing wrong with masturbating or cruising the Internet. But Bill no longer felt in control of how long or how often he engaged in these activities. His behavior controlled him, not the other way around.

Carnes says that sex addicts view the world through a sexual filter. To cope with stress and relieve himself of tension, the addict obsesses on sexual fantasies and sexualizes his every experience. To get through a stressful day at the office, a sex addict may depart into fantasies and thereby distract himself from his job. He may even misinterpret coworkers' behavior as come-ons. But that's how life appears to him through his sexual filter.

When clients deny that their sex lives have *become* their lives, I help them track themselves more closely. While at work, in the classroom, or during a tense time in their relationship, do they set aside time to hook up with somebody or view pornography? Eventually they recognize why this kind of behavior counts as sexual obsession. Even without an explicit fantasy, just making sure everything else is out of the way constitutes a preoccupation with sex and sexual fantasy.

Of course, planning for a sexual experience ahead of time isn't by itself a sign of addiction. I look for regular patterns. Does a client prefer fantasy to real-life intimacy? Are the planning and the chase distractions from daily stress? I've treated high-powered attorneys and busy financial planners who needed to masturbate in the men's room or under the desk in their private offices to get through the day.

The essence of any addiction is using behavior to banish unwanted feelings and thoughts. The self-soothing hit of PEA and other biochemicals like adrenaline and endorphins gives temporary relief from anxiety and depression. But when the sexual behavior is over, the sex addict's mood will drop into shame, depression, and often despair at having indulged his obsessions and compulsions yet again.

Sex often lets us act out feelings about whoever we're with—or about ourselves. In other words, we try to resolve feelings and memories we can't express consciously by acting them out at an unconscious level. In this way every new hook-up soothes some issue that's been eating at the sex addict for years. For his recovery, he needs to explore this unconscious process.

My goal—and my clients'—is to identify behavior that is objectively healthy, as well as behavior that's not. Sex addicts might prefer a series of anonymous partners to one ongoing, intimate love relationship. (Think about the huge difference between *having sex* and *making love*.) As we've learned, a sex addict often finds that anonymous encounters interfere with the love and companionship he really desires. So when a client claims he prefers one anonymous encounter after another, I often ask, "Is this what you really want?"

It's often easier to give in to compelling urges than to try to combat them. We easily fool ourselves into thinking that whatever we're already doing is what we want. We're reluctant to do some soul-searching to ensure that's really so.

From time to time almost every man, partnered or single, finds himself spinning sexual fantasies and imagining an anonymous encounter. But this fantasizing is short-lived. It doesn't interfere with his life or keep him from pursuing the one relationship that's central to his happiness. Like Bill, the sex addict's priorities block him from achieving most other worthwhile goals.

Let's look closely at the boundaries between healthy and unhealthy behaviors. Some of the behaviors Carnes identifies as Sexual Acting Out (SAO, for short) include:

Compulsive masturbation. There's no normative frequency. Nor is it "self abuse," as it was called in the 1940s and '50s. In an old joke, a father tells his son that if he masturbates he'll go blind. The kid responds, "Can I do it until I need glasses?" The sex addict won't stop until his penis is sore or abraded and there's no more ejaculate left. Or he may jerk off in his car, in a park, or a rest room with the hope of being seen. He prefers do-it-yourself sex to the challenge of wooing and winning a partner. Or, if partnered, he has little sexual energy left, and the relationship diminishes.

Overindulgence in pornography. Do you use porn to boost or assist your sex life? No problem! But do you prefer photos to a man who walks and talks? Do you *need* porn to get aroused and reach orgasm? Are other forms of lovemaking not quite as satisfying?

Exhibitionism. Yes, this *is* a problem. For years, society has allowed women to sport scooped tops and revealing miniskirts. Nowadays, men can be show-offs too. Younger guys wear net shirts and pants down around their pelvic bones.

Brad Pitt has appeared twice on the cover of *Vanity Fair* magazine. First time, he was pensive and moody, fully clothed, ready to light up a cigarette. The next time, he was grinning, with his shirt wide open, flashing his pecs and abs. The photographer? The late Herb Ritts, who made a career of snapping young, smooth-chested Abercrombie & Fitch types wearing as little as possible.

Strippers of both sexes get paid to show off their bodies to turn on whoever's watching. In gay nightclubs, performers gyrate and strip down while patrons stuff dollar bills into the performers' socks or jockstraps. Exhibitionists are just the opposite. They show off their bodies (or more often, just their genitals) to turn *themselves* on. An exhibitionist's thrill depends on his onlooker's reactions. The straight flasher gets a high from exposing himself and shocking women—the equivalent of visual rape.

Some gay men drive around bare-chested—even totally naked— and post their exact itinerary on chat rooms. Waste of time and gas? Not if you're an exhibitionist!

At night, after going to the bars, Trevor would take off all his clothes and, at stoplights, display his erection to male drivers in cars beside him. Often these men became angry and chased him. He'd speed away, knowing he might find himself in serious trouble if they caught him. But the thrill of danger made Trevor persist in his behavior.

While traveling for business, another client frequented bath-houses across the country. He enjoyed fellatio and anal sex with anonymous bottoms. One time he noticed an abrasion on his penis. Even so, that night he let a number of men orally service him at a bathhouse. Moving on to unprotected anal sex, he suddenly became concerned about HIV. Looking down at the man, he asked, "You're not HIV-positive, are you?" The man looked up at him and said, "Aren't we all?"

My client immediately snapped out of his sexual trance, left the bathhouse, and worried nonstop as he waited for his HIV results to come back. Why had he acted this way, knowing that a sore on his penis (a possible STD symptom in itself) increases the risk of HIV? A sex addict minimizes consequences and in doing so overlooks even obvious risks.

Voyeurism. Again, simply observing another man having sex isn't a problem in itself. Going to the baths, sex parties, and Web-cam sites are perfectly legitimate ways to watch other men who like to be watched. But sex addicts push the envelope and pose offense to others and risk to themselves. They'll secretly videotape others, drill peepholes in public bathrooms, or loiter to watch the men who enter these facilities.

Checking out the guy at the urinal next to you isn't necessarily a sign of sexual addiction. If straight men could urinate next to women, the women would peek too! But for a sex addict, this activity can consume an entire afternoon. He may even leave work early to hit the local rest rooms, putting his life on hold.

Compulsive cybersex. On the Internet, someone can Instant-Message someone else to initiate sex talk. If the other person begs off but the instigator persists, this is abuse.

Typically, the sex addict prefers quick online sex to the challenge of negotiating with a possible partner. He'll spend hours (and lots of money) online, viewing Internet porn, scanning personal ads, and frequenting chat rooms. Family and friends may be watching TV in the same room while he views porn Web sites on his laptop. If someone glances over at what he's doing, he can switch to a different screen with the click of the mouse. Cybersex doesn't have to be associated with masturbation. The chase and the hunt are more exciting than the catch.

Patrick Carnes writes about the "addictive cycle." During the *pre-occupation* stage, a sex addict makes sure he has enough time and money to go to bars or clubs. He plans his day, even his week, around his hunt for sex.

In *ritualization*, the addict frequents the same bars and clubs, wearing the same clothes or cologne, and behaves in similar ways each time. Unconsciously, most sex addicts prefer preoccupation and ritualization to actual sex because after orgasm they "crash" into the last stage: despair. To relieve their depression, they start the cycle over again.

Matt, in his 30s, was arrested for soliciting an undercover officer in a public park. After a thorough assessment of his history, I warned Matt that his behavior suggested sexual addiction. He was offended: "You're a snobbish gay man who looks down on the gay community you don't understand." Matt's quest for anonymous sex was "just part of the culture. That's the way it is!"

Matt spent hours at rest stops hanging out with friends and cruising for sexual activity. (Notice that this accords with Carnes's preoccupation and ritualization stages.) I reminded Matt that undercover police patrol rest areas and that bathhouses are raided on a regular basis. "I have a right to be there," he retorted. "The cops are on a witch hunt." He blamed them for setting up entrapments at public rest rooms.

Gently, I explained that he was placing himself at risk, knowing full well that he might be arrested. When I tried to educate him on the definition and dynamics of sexual addiction, he became enraged. "That's a label! Another way to snuff out gay sexuality."

Many gay men have been oppressed for so long that they suspect—and usually reject—any attempt to restrain their sexual expression. Matt didn't last long in treatment because he didn't want to be accountable for his sexual behavior.

True, police set up stings to arrest men for soliciting sex or for "public lewdness." Entrapment is definitely an issue: Undercover officers encourage gay men to expose their genitals before they whip out the handcuffs. Crackdowns typically occur before a local election. In one major city, the police department has an unofficial program for arresting cruisers that they call "Bag-a-Fag." I tell clients, "You know that public behavior can get you locked up! Why go back there, time and again?"

These days, we gay men have so many more ways to meet one another. Why not volunteer at a gay organization where you can meet responsible guys rather than place yourself at risk of arrest or gay bashing?

Gay men who aren't fully out—many of them still married to women—go underground. While I don't condone anonymous sexual activity in parks and rest areas, I do think it evolved in the first place because gay culture has been marginalized in so many ways. There are no social conventions that allow us to mature sexually in healthy ways. In the movie *Philadelphia*, a straight attorney named Joe Miller (Denzel Washington) represents a gay man named Andrew Beckett (Tom Hanks) in a civil suit after Andrew is unfairly fired because he has AIDS. In a drugstore, a gay man recognizes the lawyer, strikes up a conversation, and praises him for the work he's done on the case. Then—with a woman in same aisle eavesdropping—he asks Joe out on a date. Joe says, "What, you think I'm gay? Do I look gay to you?" The gay male—in basketball attire, having come from a game—retorts, "Do I look gay to *you?*"

Joe, humiliated because the onlooker in the aisle has seen this all, grabs the basketball player and says, "I ought to kick your faggoty ass!" This is an excellent example of how gay men are at risk when they flirt with men who might be straight. We're pushed underground, where other guys are likely to be interested. And if they're not, they won't harm us. The fact that men cruise toilets attests to the fact that, perhaps unconsciously, they view sex as "dirty." That said, each of us remains responsible for his own actions—and for the risks that he knowingly assumes.

Carnes says that the sexual addict suffers from four erroneous core beliefs:

1. I am basically bad and unworthy.
2. No one will love me as I am.
3. My needs will never be met if I have to rely on others.
4. Sex is my most important need.

He adds that a high percentage of sex addicts have been sexually abused. Based on my clients' reports, I agree—though not all sexually addicted men were sexually abused. The *type* of abuse is important. In overt abuse, there's little doubt about the nature of the act. Covert abuse—including sexualized hugs that take too long—is usually more subtle and often leaves the victim wondering whether abuse really occurred. But the damage is done, and it always registers on an unconscious level: Clients often tell me they feel uncomfortable and "icky" around the perpetrator.

Awareness of a parent's having an affair also counts as covert abuse. A child shouldn't be exposed to that information. (Of course, the affair shouldn't be happening at all.) In some families, mothers give their sons the message that women are more moral and civilized, while men are bad and hurtful. This gender-bashing is also covert sexual abuse. Other examples include name-calling ("You're a sissy"), inappropriate comments on a child's pubertal development, and deliberate exposure to adult nudity.

In another form of covert abuse, parents try to turn their children into partners—typically, when a husband neglects his wife's needs. I see this syndrome a lot with gay men and their mothers. To reiterate: This isn't what makes the boy gay. But because gay boys are more sensitive, verbal, and approachable, many mothers turn to their gay sons for the kind of emotional support that only an adult should provide. A very good book on this topic is Pat Love's *Emotional Incest Syndrome: When a Parent's Love Rules Your Life.* Love discusses the emotional abuse that occurs when a mother—or father—becomes too dependent on a child.[4] Another good book on this topic is

Kenneth Adam's *Silently Seduced: When Parents Make Their Children Partners—Understanding Covert Incest.*[5]

Very often, sex addicts habitually repeat their original childhood abuse. If a boy is abused and tells about it, responsible adults can help him understand that the abuse isn't his fault. But if a boy's abused and says nothing—or if he does tell and nobody offers help—there's double damage: the abuse and the lack of responsiveness from others. This leaves him feeling silenced in his suffering and feeling like nobody cares. This can make the trauma worse. His unconscious seeks other ways to resolve the abuse because it wasn't adequately cared for in the first place.

Some men come into my office believing they're gay as a result of childhood sexual abuse. Not true! Abuse shapes behavior, not orientation, for gays and heterosexuals alike. In his first appointment, a straight man I once treated said he was "queered" by his brother during his childhood. When Jesse was 10, his 15-year-old brother told him, "Your penis has to be examined." Then his older brother fondled his genitals. This went on for years. Later, Jesse became a sexual addict, exposing himself to women in malls, parking lots, even parties at work, and inviting them to "examine" him.

Once we identified and resolved his original sexual abuse by his brother, Jesse stopped acting out. He was able to be monogamous with his wife and no longer felt compelled to have other women "examine" him. Though another male molested him, this abuse didn't shape his sexual or romantic orientation. But it did shape his homophobia! Our therapy included understanding that what his brother did to him was all about power and control. There was nothing "queer" or "gay" about it.

Walt was arrested for public indecency after flashing an undercover police officer in a public rest room. Walt had been doing this throughout his adult sexual life. In therapy, he also disclosed that he wasn't happy with his partner. He found his emotional love waning and his lust wandering elsewhere.

Throughout their relationship, Walt had frequented rest areas and rest rooms in malls and airports, without his partner knowing about it. Because he preferred cruising to spending time with his partner, he assumed their relationship was over.

During our work together, I suggested that his relationship might actually be in fine shape. I asked whether his sexual behavior might be the root of his problem. Was he giving his relationship enough of a chance? Despite his unhappiness, Walt defended his behavior. He enjoyed the risk as well as the novelty of sex with new men he met.

In exploring his childhood, Walt recalled his grandfather giving him a bath at the age of 6. The grandfather washed Walt's penis and scrotum for an unusually long time. Finally Walt asked, "Why are you doing that?" His grandfather said his penis was dirty and needed extra attention. Walt dried off, dressed, and went downstairs to tell his grandmother, who dismissed the whole issue. Walt never visited his grandparents alone again. Nor did he ever discuss the incident with his parents.

He was left without any resolution and needed validation: someone to tell him that his grandfather had done wrong and that telling his grandmother had been the right thing to do. After Walt grew up, he frequented public bathrooms and rest areas. He jerked off with strangers and enjoyed oral sex through glory holes. He wasn't interested in meeting men online, in bars, or in clubs.

I helped him understand the connection: His grandfather had molested him in a bathroom. Now, his unconscious—having received no resolution to the trauma—was "telling about it" through compulsive sexual behavior. Walt agreed that his addictive sexual behavior was a direct result of his grandfather's abuse.

Walt eventually told his partner about his arrest and about what he had learned in therapy. Walt's partner tried to help him by being creative. They put up a drywall "stall," drilled a glory hole, and engaged in oral sex. Walt found this a turn-on. For a while, this private glory hole—and the legal charges hanging over his head— helped him resist his urge to cruise. He and his partner began to work on their relationship while Walt explored his sexual addiction.

But he didn't want to look very closely at what his grandfather had done, other than to accept that it happened and that it was linked to his sexual addiction. He wanted to "put it in the past. I want to move on." I strongly encouraged him to look at the abuse more closely to help resolve it.

I run a group for men who've been sexually abused and who are now sexually addicted. Walt declined to join the group, saying that individual therapy and periodic couples therapy with his partner was enough. Having stopped his sexual acting-out, Walt felt that he had been "cured." But after a while, the glory hole in his basement no longer gave him enough pleasure. After his legal hassles cleared, his urge for bathroom sex returned. He told me that despite his legal hassles, he wanted to keep on cruising rest areas and bathrooms because "It brings me joy."

When he finally agreed to join our group, Walt confronted my challenges and admitted he was in total relapse. He began working harder on his recovery and his relationship and ultimately became internally motivated. He no longer needed the external threat of possible legal hassles to take charge of his life.

At first, Walt wasn't ready to examine how deeply sexual abuse had affected him. His grandfather should have felt fear, shame, and anxiety about what he did. Instead, Walt took those emotions on himself and lived with those feelings to protect his perpetrator.

Mark Schwartz, a pioneer in the field of sexual addiction who works at the Master's and Johnson Treatment Center in St. Louis, defines compulsive sexual behavior as an "intimacy disorder."[6] In his view, the compulsive individual, as a child, was typically victimized by abusive, neglectful, or smothering caretakers. Lacking nurturing, the victim had to look after himself. As a result, he now equates sex with nurturing. His psyche—seeking pleasure, not pain—passes painful emotional memories through a sexual filter to make them "feel better." His passive rage is expressed as deviation or even perversion.

The sex addict hasn't developed the skills to form and maintain intimate relationships with other adults. In consequence, close relationships cause him fear, shame, and anxiety.

I agree: Sexual addiction and compulsivity are both intimacy disorders. We gay men are taught, early on, not to be intimate with one another, let alone be open to our families or classmates. Of course we have intimacy disorders! Abuse that begins early in a gay boy's life leaves him extremely susceptible to sexual addiction.

One definition of abuse is when any person dominates and exploits another—thereby violating trust and the promise of protection. Someone who sees himself as "in control" uses his status to manipulate, misuse, degrade, humiliate, or even hurt others—who, by inference, are always inferior. Many studies have confirmed that the basic motivation for rape is power, not sex. Other forms of sexual abuse follow the same pathology.

The sexual abuser's ideal target is a child who's still naive, lacking the "immune system" imparted by emotional and intellectual experience that tells him when he's being violated—and when to resist, and when to say no. A dominant perpetrator—uncle, stepfather, or other male figure who's familiar, trusted, and seemingly all-powerful—can easily lure a boy into a sexual relationship and force him to comply.

At a conference, I spoke about how sexual abuse contributes to sexual addiction and promiscuity. Afterward, Tim—a gay man in his 50s—approached me privately to confess that all his adult sex life had taken place in public parks, where he serviced male hustlers, with no reciprocation.

Though he'd already been arrested once, after soliciting an undercover police officer, he argued that sexual promiscuity is part and parcel of being gay. I challenged him on this and said that although sexual promiscuity is part of our community, it doesn't *have* to be part of gay life.

In our therapy, he reported being severely depressed, even suicidal. I took his claims seriously, since he'd already made several attempts. Tim had trouble holding jobs; he was constantly being let go. Over the years, he'd seen several other therapists. In the course of his therapy with me, he revealed that when he was a young adult he was raped by a rugby player he picked up in a public park. The incident occurred in 1969 and continued to shape his daily life.

I asked to hear more about his early years. Tim told me that when he was a child, an older male cousin had sodomized him—which he didn't label as rape or even as abuse. When his alcoholic father learned of this, he forbade Tim ever to see his cousin again. "That behavior's sick. You better not be a damned queer," Tim's father told him. Early on, Tim's father shamed him for being insufficiently masculine, for not "being a man."

Tim's cruel father handed Tim a defective lovemap, which led him to seek men who would treat him with the same indifference his father had. His low self-esteem had never recovered from the damage his father had inflicted.

Studies report that adults who suffer rape or abuse in adulthood—or who, as perpetrators, go on to rape or abuse others—were often victims of abuse themselves. The sexually abused child grows up convinced that something's wrong with him. As an adult, he recreates familiar—even if abusive—acts of "love." I call this pattern "returning to the scene of the crime."

In Tim's case, the original offense was his father's relentless browbeating. For the rest of his life, Tim felt attracted to abusive authority figures. At first, he didn't see his older cousin's anal penetration as abuse—because he'd enjoyed it and because there wasn't any physical violence involved. Because he was attracted to his cousin, his pleasure confused him.

When a heterosexual male teen has sex with an older woman, it's like a merit badge. He can talk about his experience with his friends and get high fives. Even therapists often overlook such events, though nowadays we acknowledge them as a form of sexual abuse. As an adult, the woman is an authority figure who is responsible for protecting minors from predatory advances. Her sexual advance toward the younger male teen is abusive.

Tim had been to several psychotherapists and psychiatrists, none of whom addressed his rapes. I was the first professional ever to ask about them in detail. It took Tim weeks to describe the second one.

One night, Tim was cruising a park looking for a sexual encounter. Although gay men still cruise public parks and rest areas, most of them are closeted and sexually addicted. But back in the 1960s, there were very few other ways for gay men to find each other.

Tim found a masculine, muscular young man who had played rugby in college. Tim invited the man back home, where they began consensual fondling, kissing, and oral sex. The man tried to talk Tim into anal intercourse, but he wasn't interested. He enjoyed anal sex, passive or active, only with men for whom he felt love, and he intended this encounter to be strictly oral sex. But the man wouldn't take no for an answer. Bigger and stronger, he forced himself on Tim, with no lubrication. Tim screamed in pain, but since he lived alone there was no one to hear him. The rapist, having achieved his release, laughed, called Tim a "fucking faggot" who "deserved what he got" and left. Tim was bleeding, internally and externally, but he didn't report the assault. He was a gay man who'd cruised a public park— who'd give him sympathy?

After two days of continued bleeding forced him to call in sick at work, he phoned a friend, who urged him to go to the emergency room. Reluctantly, he did. The ER physician was stern and patronizing and asked Tim flatly, "Are you homosexual?" Tim admitted he was, whereupon the doctor treated him with disdain—reinforcing the rugby player's assertion that he "deserved" what he got. The doctor put Tim in stirrups to examine his injuries and inserted a speculum forcibly and carelessly into Tim's anus, causing further injury. Tim was too embarrassed to protest.

For nine months Tim sat on an inflatable plastic donut designed for patients recovering from hemorrhoid surgery. He needed special baths and ointments to recover from the rape and the further injuries that the ER doctor inflicted.

Each of these three episodes was rape. It took Tim years before he could talk about the rugby player in group therapy. Often, when recalling what had happened, he'd fall silent and tell us he'd "had enough"—a decision I honored every time. The rugby player and the doctor had stolen Tim's control. Now I wanted him to feel in control of his story and his entire life. In one group session, Tim began to shake and cry so much that I asked all the other members to physically hold him and offer him comfort and support.

In another group session, Tim said that now, when he recalled the rapes, he remembers it was like looking down on himself from the ceiling while the rape was happening. This kind of dissociation is common among people who are being traumatized sexually. When their psyches later recall the trauma, they dissociate all over again in different ways to "numb" the painful feelings. Dissociation is a form of anesthesia for the victim. The unconscious later tries to resolve the trauma by returning to the scene of the crime, ironically. However, for sex addicts, or anyone else for that matter, dissociative behavior doesn't solve—or resolve—the original crime. In vain attempts to heal themselves, men like Tim withdraw into sexual behavior to prevent anxiety and terrible memories from intruding into their lives.

Mark Schwartz suggests that during sexual abuse, victims experience high levels of fear but also excitement.[7] Later, as their sexuality develops, they tend to recreate those same elements through compulsive behavior. Just as the original abuse was unwanted, so is the compulsion—perfectly mirroring the original abuse. Such was the case with Tim, whose experience provides a perfect example of how sexual abuse—overt and covert—perpetuates itself in the life of the victims.

I help gay men begin to ease into recovery from sexual compulsion by having them recognize that their behavior is compulsive. Once that's established, I do a thorough evaluation of their childhood history and early caregivers. I ask about abuse of any kind—physical, emotional, neglect—and explain what each one is. I let the client know the various pathways we can follow to get him back to health.

I think your sexual behavior and fantasies are windows into who you are. In other words, whatever gives you the greatest pleasure sexually tells a lot about you. Sexuality is an extension of our inner core, always telling a story—if not on a conscious level.

In an excellent episode of the Showtime series *Queer as Folk*, Emmett masturbates while typing online and using his screen name PITTS9X6. His profile describes him as big, smooth, 6-foot-2, 195 pounds, 4% body fat, and uncut. His tells his friend Ted about his frustration at not being able to meet "usemyhole27," with whom he's been having cybersex. Ted encourages Emmett to tell the guy the truth. Emmett responds by saying, "What? Tell him I'm a big nellie bottom who wishes he was a beefy, brutal top?"

In another scene, Emmett is about to delete his screen name PITTS9X6. Just as he is about to click the Delete button a big, smooth, 6-foot-2, 195-pound, 4% body fat male appears in his apartment, identifying himself as PITTS9X6. He pulls down his pants to reveal his uncut "9X6." Emmett, in disbelief, thinks he's going crazy, but soon realizes that this figment of his overactive imagination has come to life.

PITTS9X6 doesn't want Emmett to delete him. Instead, his screen name makes him a deal: "If I could make you a big beefy top rather than a nellie bottom, will you let me live?"

"They want you, the fantasy," says Emmett. "Not me, the real person." The screen name assures him that he can help Emmett become more like his false persona.

"But I'm not like you," says Emmett.

"I came from somewhere, didn't I?" the screen name replies.

The rest of the episode shows how PITTS9X6 teaches Emmett to find the big beefy top within and be more like him. Ultimately, Emmett steps into his other persona and finds that he really can be the beefy top he portrays online.

This is an excellent depiction of how sexual acting-out tells a story about who we are—or who we want to be. Most men don't need to examine that story, since their sexual behavior doesn't interfere with their lives. But for those struggling with sexual compulsion, decoding sexual acting-out is extremely helpful.

Nathan, 27, entered therapy with me after his boyfriend, whom he'd dated for two years, began an affair and ended their relationship. After that, Nate's sexual acting out increased. After hours of phone sex, he ran up hundreds of dollars in credit card debt. When I asked about his sexual behaviors and fantasies, he was highly embarrassed. I explained that if he didn't tell me, we couldn't get to the core of whatever was driving his behavior.

Nate called phone-sex numbers and asked men to humiliate him by telling him he had a small penis and that he "wasn't a man." He'd ask the guy to laugh at him and tell him that he was going to fuck another man in front of him and together they would laugh. In the fantasy, the two men would demand that Nathan masturbate while he watched to further humiliate him.

Nate was troubled primarily because he preferred this fantasy to healthy, loving sexual play. A "nice" man just role-playing this scene for fun wasn't satisfying. Nathan preferred men who deliberately treated him badly, which helped him have better orgasm and sexual arousal. He found himself masturbating to the image of his ex-boyfriend having sex with his new lover while both of them laughed at Nate.

Nathan couldn't identify any sexual abuse in his past. He did have one memory that haunted him: When he was between 4 and 7 years old, he and his family often watched television together. His mother would slip her hand into Nathan's pants, fondle his bare bottom, and tell him "what a nice cute little butt" he had. His father and older brother laughed at the routine. Nathan knew he didn't like it and told his mother so, but she persisted and his father did nothing to stop it. It became normal behavior.

When I explained that this was, in fact, sexual abuse, Nathan found my assertion incredibly difficult to believe. No one wants to believe he's the victim of incest, or that his mother was the perpetrator. Again, it's too scary to believe that your own caretakers are dangerous and harmful—particularly your mother! It feels safer to blame yourself and defend your abuser.

Now, looking at Nate's sexual acting-out, we could see the pattern of his instant replay. His need to be laughed at mirrored his need to return to when he *was* young and small, when his family's lovemap had included laughter and humiliation as his mother held his buttocks. From a little boy's perspective, his mother had betrayed him by seducing him with her hand on his buttocks, then going to bed with his father. This played out in his humiliation fantasy, where his partner preferred another man—mirroring the loss of control Nate had felt as a child. Though a woman had abused him, he wanted men to humiliate him, because he was gay. He was oriented toward men, not women.

Nathan entered both individual and group therapy—both were necessary to heal his sexual addiction. In group, Nathan saw hetero-sexual men struggling with similar incest issues related to their own mothers. Significantly, abuse hadn't affected Nate's sexual and roman-tic orientation. Listening to the other men in his group helped him feel validated and believe that what his mother had done was wrong.

Sexually abused children ask, "What did I do to deserve this? What made them know they could do it?" Recovering from sexual addiction requires that the truth be exposed, no matter how difficult. Nate's sexual behaviors continued and, during our work, actually increased. This isn't uncommon: The purpose of sexual addiction is to help repress painful memories. The more we uncovered, the more acutely Nate felt the pull of his addiction.

It took Nathan years to accept these insights and come to terms with them, but once he did he was able to make progress in his recov-ery. When he finally saw the connections, he had to decide what to do about them. He worried we were going to make his mother out to be a monster—a common therapeutic concern that I'll cover more fully in Chapter 7. I assured him this was not the direction his ther-apy was going. However, he did need to learn to stop defending his mother and making himself out to be the problem.

Nathan followed the recommendations he received in his 12 Step group: He blocked the 900 numbers he'd called to engage in phone sex, and he stopped going online. Still, he found ways to bypass the 900 block and, during masturbation, engaged his fantasy more fever-ishly than ever.

Part of Nathan's treatment was to confront his mother and father. Some men decide to do this in reality. Others decide to expend this repressed anger by writing letters they never send, talking about it extensively in therapy, or role-playing. Nate asked other group members to play his mother and father while he prac-ticed telling them how he felt about what happened to him in childhood. In group, he worked out his anger through experiential exercises (which I'll explain in Chapter 7). Nathan grew close to the men in his group and formed healthy attachments to them. He was able to express his feelings and confront other members when he felt in conflict with them.

The goal for them all was to practice with one another healthy relational skills that they could take out into the real world and use in their interactions with friends and future partners. Ultimately, Nathan was able to establish a loving relationship with a man who treated him appropriately. He was even able to recreate his humiliation fantasy with this partner and have fun with it—in respectful, non-self-defeating ways.

Some therapists might assume that Nathan hadn't fully recovered because he still engaged in his humiliation fantasy. I don't agree. Early childhood imprinting is hardwired and therefore very difficult to overcome, particularly when it's fused with sexual thoughts and fantasies. Nathan overcame his compulsiveness and learned to sustain a loving relationship—clear evidence of his hard work and progress in recovery.

In general, there's nothing inherently wrong with sexual fantasies, and it's important not to pathologize them. If they're not compulsive and if they're acted out in a consensual way, fantasies can be hot and exciting. However, it's important to understand that at its core sexual addiction isn't about sex. Rather, the addictive behavior has become sexualized because the unconscious is always drawn toward pleasure instead of pain. Trauma is turned into orgasm. But until the source of the trauma is resolved, the sexual reenactments never end.

Very often, clients tell me they feel "forced" to engage in their compulsive sexual behavior, as if they had no choice. They literally feel they'll die or be unable to get through their day. This is because the compulsion to act out mimics the original sexual abuse forced upon the child. As a little boy, Nathan couldn't stop his mother from slipping her hand down his pants. He couldn't escape abuse, and he felt he couldn't escape his later sexual compulsion.

According to the lovemap theory, children are geniuses at finding ways to code their pain. (Nathan's unconscious found a brilliant way to protect his mother and cover up her crime.) Within the sexual acting-out, behaviors become metaphors for the past. Many theorists believe that strong elements of anger, even rage, underlie sexual compulsion as a consequence of the shame that sexual addicts feel about themselves.

In groups and workshops for gay men, I often ask, "Where's our anger about how we are treated?" Lesbians express their indignation directly at sexism and heterosexism and often take political action, but I don't see this as much in the gay male community. In both individual and group therapy, I urge clients to express their anger in firm, appropriate, and healing ways. For example: When a college instructor expressed homophobia, a gay student client outed himself and stated that he didn't appreciate listening to the man's nonsense.

In *Sexual Addiction: An Integrated Approach,* Aviel Goodman cites a study that suggests sexual behaviors are sustained by "mood-dependent motives." In short, if sexual addiction is driven by emotions, medication can help manage the mood disorder and thereby eliminate the behavior. Clearly, libido drives the sexually addictive behavior, and some medications—including Prozac, Zoloft, Paxil, and Celexa—help to lower sex drive as well as to improve mood. Other medications Goodman reports as helpful include Luvox, Tofranil, Norpramine, Anafranil, Lithium, and Buspar.[8] In any case, clients should consult a psychiatrist or general physician before beginning treatment with these drugs.

Clients worry that if they start taking a medication they'll have to take it for life, which makes them want to postpone drug therapies until they try every other route first. I support that decision, though I have observed that clients struggling with sexual addiction generally find it helpful to be on *something*—not to numb their emotions but to stabilize them. This stability affords them the space to decode their sexual behavior without triggering strong feelings that would only cause them to relapse.

Unfortunately, relapse is part of recovery. A man can avoid drugs and alcohol, but not his own genitals! The victim of an eating disorder can't stop feeling hungry, nor can a sex addict stop feeling horny.

Sex is part of our biology, so relapses are more likely to be part of the recovery among sex addicts.

Still, it's wise to avoid people, places, or situations that might encourage relapse. Early in recovery, I counsel clients to make a list of those risky factors. They're different for every individual, and you will swiftly learn what they are. But I help clients understand that if they do relapse, it's not the end of the world. They can learn from their relapse. I am not saying, "Go ahead, relapse, and let's learn from it." But predicting it as part of the recovery, particularly early on, heads off feelings of shame and failure.

After a relapse, always track back to the events or experiences that led up to it. Most sex addicts say, "I don't know how this happened." They really mean it. Life isn't an erotic episode of *Bewitched,* in which you magically end up back in the bathhouse, rest area, or on the Internet. Sex addicts make all kinds of small decisions, many totally unconscious, to get to the sexual acting-out behaviors.

Look back and see. Examine where and when you decided to:

1. Make sure you had enough time to hook up.
2. Blow off the afternoon.
3. Make sure you had enough to pay for the theater or bathhouse.
4. "Innocently" go on line or scan personal ads that prompted you to find this willing, anonymous partner.
5. Make plans to meet this guy.
6. Tell yourself "A few more minutes won't hurt," then find yourself online all night.

Communication is another key element in recovery. Isolation prevents friends, family, and would-be partners from helping you. Recovery demands that you have people and sponsors who can challenge your thoughts and support you in staying on track.

There are also some specific cultural and psychological considerations: A large part of our gay culture supports your right to do whatever you want, sexually, with no restraint. This, as AA calls it, is "Stinkin' Thinking," and it can only hinder your recovery. It's easy to feel left out if you can't do "what all the other guys are doing." Plenty of places within the community aren't overly sexualized. Getting out and finding them is a necessary step.

A double life is what sexual addiction is all about. A man presents one face in public and acts out sexually in private. No one else knows both sides of him. This reflects the psychology of a man who's still closeted or not out in all situations. Being conscious and intentional about what you're doing is very important. Otherwise, your addiction can slip back in, believing it has a place in the "other" life you're living.

Attending Sex Addict Anonymous meetings for heterosexuals may be counterproductive, because it offers the gay man an escape hatch. He's able to hide among heterosexuals, who can't really help him and who won't recognize when he's on the way to relapse because they don't know the intricacies of being gay. The opposite can be equally true: They could warn you you're in slippery territory because you're doing something that, for a gay man, is perfectly legitimate. Better to look for Sexual Compulsives Anonymous meetings, which are predominantly for gay men.

Various 12 Step meetings are available to sex addicts, but it's vital to recognize the fundamental differences between Sex Addicts Anonymous, Sex and Love Addicts Anonymous, Sexual Compulsives Anonymous, and Sexaholics Anonymous.

Sex Addicts Anonymous (SAA) is most liberal in letting you define your own sexual boundaries. SAA welcomes everybody: men, women, gay, straight, bi-attractional, and others. They tend to focus on paraphilias, in which arousal and gratification depend on fantasizing about—and engaging in—sexual behavior that's atypical and extreme.

Paraphiliacs fixate on a particular act, like inflicting or receiving pain and/or humiliation, or on fetishes, like shoes, feet, and underwear. Ads offering soiled jockstraps and used underwear are rife in many gay publications, and can be found just as easily on eBay. Again, enjoying a fetish isn't the problem. Compulsivity and a preference for fetishism over a full sexual relationship with another human being *are* problematic.

Sex and Love Addicts Anonymous (SLAA) focuses on love addiction—an insatiable craving for that "in love with love," PEA infatuation high. Love addicts seek the lightning-bolt, blown-away, "love at first sight" kick. Again, men and women, gay, straight, and bi-attractional people are all welcome. Unlike SAA meetings, where the majority of participants are men, SLAA meetings attract more women who, in our society, tend to focus on the relational, loving side of their relationships.

This program helps men and women who tend to move from one honeymoon to another—as soon as troubles arise, they move on, hoping that a new relationship will provide what the last one failed to deliver.

Then there's *Sexaholics Anonymous* (SA). Their rigid, orthodox, cookie-cutter approach requires participants to accept that no sexual relations should occur outside marriage. Leaders tell participants what their recovery and sobriety should look like: "Any form of sex with one's self or with partners other than the spouse is progressively addictive and destructive." I say decide for yourself what works and what doesn't! Not surprisingly, many gay clients tell me they feel excluded from this particular group.

Sexual Compulsives Anonymous (SCA) split from Sexaholics Anonymous because some gay men felt uncomfortable with SA's fundamentalist, heterosexist overtones. Members of SCA design their recovery program along the lines of SAA. In these groups, gay men can discuss their special needs and talk openly and honestly. Lesbians and heterosexuals are welcome, but most members are gay males.

Sexual addiction prevents its sufferers from forming deep relationships. That's why it's so important to have another person to relate to on a nonsexual level. Time and again, studies show that for the best results, the sexual addict should engage in individual, group, and 12 Step programs simultaneously. In the company of others, he's forced to develop his intimacy and relationship skills.

Given that sexual addiction is an intimacy disorder, it makes sense that the best, most healing "therapy" of all is an adult love relationship, which demands a level of emotional commitment that casual hook-ups can never duplicate. Imago Relationship Therapy teaches that since we were originally wounded in relationships, healing can only take place in the context of a mature, intimate relationship.

References

1. Patrick Carnes, *Out of the Shadows: Understanding Sexual Addiction* (3rd edition). Center City, MN: Hazelden Information Education (May 1, 2001).

2. Eli Coleman, *Case Studies in Sex Therapy*, edited by Raymond C. Rosen and Sandra R. Leiblum. New York: Guilford Publications (1995).

3. John Money, *Lovemaps: Clinical Concepts of Sexual/Erotic Health and Pathology, Paraphilia, and Gender Transposition in Childhood, Adolescence, and Maturity.* New York: Irvington Publishers (1986).

4. Pat Love, *Emotional Incest Syndrome: When a Parent's Love Rules Your Life.* New York: Bantam Books (1990).

5. Kenneth M. Adams, *Silently Seduced: When Parents Make Their Children Partners—Understanding Covert Incest.* Deerfield Beach, FL: Health Communications, Inc. (1991).

6. Mark Schwartz and William Masters, "Integration of Trauma-based, Cognitive, Behavioral, Systematic, and Addiction Approaches for Treatment of Hypersexual Pair-Bonding Disorder," *Sexual Addiction and Compulsivity: The Journal of Treatment and Prevention*, Volume 1, 1994.

7. Ibid.

8. Aviel Goodman, *Sexual Addiction: An Integrated Approach.* Madison, CT: International Universities Press (1998).

Chapter 6
Learn From Successful Mentors Who've Been There, Done That

GAY, SHMAY! JUST DON'T BE ALONE.
—my grandmother

Every culture needs strong mentors.

Most of what I know of Jewish tradition was passed to me by my grandmother, my Bubbie. Though not formally educated, she knows quite a bit of Jewish religion and culture, which have guided her through her long life.

As I write this, I'm reminded that she insisted that I use her name in print. "Yusella [*Yiddish for "Joey" or "little Joe"*], when you mention me in your articles, I notice you don't say my name. Why not?"

"Bubbie," I replied, "I didn't know you *had* a name until I was in my teens. Everyone called you Bubbie. Even your friends!"

Mary helped my mother raise me and taught me why we Jews light candles on the Sabbath and keep kosher. (As a child, I was upset that she'd never know the taste of a cheeseburger or pizza with pepperoni!) A woman full of old-world family values, morality, spirituality, and holiness, she is filled with joy whenever she reconnects with her heritage. I relish her stories about coming to America from Russia—and I've videotaped her so that I will never forget her words, inflections, and personality.

Unfortunately, she taught me not only spirituality but superstition as well. Even today, when I spill salt accidentally, I automatically shake it over my shoulder three times.

I'll always have memories of this strong matriarch who taught me the Jewish way. "Just don't be alone" was her way of blessing me personally, as being both Jewish and gay.

At age 13 I had my bar mitzvah. As the joke goes, "Today, I'm a man! Tomorrow, eighth grade!" Though really still a boy, I was initiated into manhood through prayer and celebration.

As gay men, we don't often receive other people's blessings. Very few mentors come forward to guide gay and lesbian youth. A lesbian comic once joked that as a girl, her role models were Dr. Smith on *Lost in Space* and Ms. Hathaway on *The Beverly Hillbillies*! What kind of gay and lesbian role models are they?

I always feel grief when an older man—in his 50s, 60s, even 70s—asks me (because I am out) what gay culture is like. It should be the other way around! In gay and lesbian culture, our identity is formed in adulthood, and we must mentor one another and ourselves.

Some very wonderful things characterize gay culture.

One: We're not bound by gender roles. When we're partnered, stereotypical expectations don't exist. Everything has to be negotiated—just as it should be in any relationship. We get to decide what works best for us.

Most male partners have been groomed to be breadwinners and providers. So who vacuums and takes out the garbage? Partnered women have been raised to nurture and make a home. At least one woman in a lesbian couple has to go out and work!

Two: We tend to explore and examine our sexuality more openly than heterosexuals. Heterosexism and homophobia have forced us to talk about our sexuality and develop a language for it. Many heterosexuals, both male and female, have difficulty knowing what they want, let alone talking about their desires.

Three: Gay culture is very honest. I think our best features are courage, assertiveness, and affirmation. It takes bravery and sincerity to come out of the closet in a society that would rather we stay passive and dishonest.

When we are honest enough to come out, others become honest

with us as well. It forces truth to the forefront for all. In the movie *In and Out,* Kevin Kline portrays a gay man. In one scene, his mother tells her girlfriends her son is gay. At that, her girlfriends decide to take risks, be honest with one another, and "come out" about their own deep, dark secrets. It illustrates what happens when we—and those around us—really tell the truth.

Unfortunately, a gay man's initiation into manhood is usually purely sexual. Society doesn't approve of an older gay man's nonsexual contact with a younger boy or teen because people assume that *sexual* contact is all the elder wants. So when a young gay man reaches his 20s, his initiation into gay culture is through sexuality—often in relation to a "mentor" he'll never see again. Just coming out, not sure of himself, he hasn't learned it's OK to approach a gay man nonsexually. So he goes the secretive, anonymous route—to rest areas, "cruisy" bathrooms, online chat rooms, or gay bars. To me, this is so sad. If older and younger gay men could gather in groups and sit down for tea and coffee, how different things would be!

In *Gay Spirit Warrior: An Empowerment Workbook for Men Who Love Men,* John Stowe writes, "Imagine a society different from our own, in which older gay men are treated with honor. Imagine a Council of Gay Elders who sit together in order to share wisdom and advice with the entire Tribe. Imagine going to this Council—being sent by your parents, even—the moment you first recognized your attraction to other men. Imagine sharing your concerns with a silver-haired mentor, a man like yourself who loves other men and who listens to you with respect. Imagine how you'd feel about yourself if you could call on this man's guidance, insight, humor, and perspective whenever you need it."[1]

I want to help something like this happen. Society may not give us permission, but you can always give yourself permission.

Jennifer, a heterosexual therapist, had a gay client, Shawn, age 17. I volunteered to come to one of their sessions to let him see what a gay male adult looks like.

Shawn, intelligent and attractive, was just starting to come out. He was scared and lonely. "Where can I find other guys my age?" he asked. "Should I tell my family and friends?" I answered his questions as best I could. A senior in high school, he was very cautious. Ultimately, Shawn told his mother, his father, and a few selected friends and teachers.

Months later, the Human Rights Campaign held its annual fundraising dinner. At the event, members of our community receive awards for their work, locally and nationally, to advance the cause of equal rights for gays and lesbians.

My partner and I had already paid to go, but I received some free tickets. I called Jennifer and asked her permission to invite Shawn and his family. I wanted him to have a positive, healthy experience in the gay community. Jennifer thought that was a great!

Shawn and his parents were thankful and honored to sit at the same table with my partner and me, along with several of our friends, both coupled and single. I was so proud to be able to show Shawn some solid role models—and show his family what gays and lesbians could achieve. Shawn's mother knew one of the award recipients, and I spoke to her at length about mothering a gay son.

The night was a success! One of my friends at the table made friends with Shawn and his parents. Later, he went to lunch with them and told me that he too wanted to help mentor this young man and his family.

Care, love, and wisdom are formed in us by the time we reach middle age. We want to share them with the younger generations. In his book *Childhood and Society*, Erik Erikson says, "Mature man needs to be needed, and maturity needs guidance as well as encouragement from what has been produced and must be taken care of. Generativity, then, is primarily the concern in establishing and guiding the next generation."[2] Younger people need guidance and mentoring, and older people want to mentor. It's human nature, and psychologically necessary.

At one of my workshops for gay men, a 25-year-old named Robb approached me. He felt uncomfortable around another workshop participant—Greg, 60, who'd been out all his life. Robb was just coming out, was new to attending gay events, and feared Greg wanted to prey on him sexually.

"Why do you think Greg is coming on to you?" I asked. Robb said it was the way Greg looked at him and the things he said. Greg had told Robb about his own coming out, 40 years before, and how different things were today. Greg complimented Robb on his bravery, told him he was very good-looking and charming, and asked Robb to go out for a coffee some time. Greg hugged Robb to welcome him into the workshop and the gay community. Robb felt that he was trying to create a romantic and sexual relationship.

At my workshops, participants have opportunities to resolve conflicts with others. I told Robb that I'd invite him to talk to Greg, and I'd help.

After they learned the communication process, Robb asked whether Greg was open to hearing his concerns—and Greg agreed. Robb explained all that he had told me: that he was uncomfortable, frustrated, and angry because he felt Greg was coming on to him.

When Robb finished, it was Greg's turn to respond. He was shocked by Robb's judgments and reactions. Greg had never thought for a minute about pursuing Robb sexually or romantically. Greg recalled feeling alone and lacking guidance from men in the gay community when he was a young man. He wanted to offer Robb a different experience, and that was all.

Robb began to cry. He said he appreciated what Greg was doing and was sorry he'd misunderstood. Robb had gone to various gay bars and rest areas where older men preyed on him and had thought Greg was doing the same. Both men began to weep. In fact, there wasn't a dry eye in the room.

I'm not exempt from wanting a gay mentor. I've always been a fan of Brian McNaught, whose several books include *On Being Gay* (written in 1975!), *Gays in the Workplace*, and *Now That I Am Out, What Do I Do?* He's a Detroit native, widely respected here and around the country. A few years ago, Mike and I were on vacation in Provincetown when I spotted McNaught. I felt like a fan after a rock star's autograph!

Anxious and overwhelmed, I consulted my partner about what to do. Even Oprah talks about how we should take a moment to thank the person who's been a role model and paved the way for our journeys. Finally I decided to approach Brian and tell him how much he'd meant to me and that his work inspired my own. He was very gracious, gave me his card, and told me to keep in touch.

I was elated. On returning home, I sent him a few of my writings. He responded with a handwritten note saying that he'd read each of my articles and enjoyed them. That meant so much to me—and I feel I am standing on his shoulders today.

A friend in his 60s had been partnered for more than 20 years, until his partner died. My friend is a vessel of wisdom about the joys and challenges of gay relationships. I still do what's right for me, of course, but I need his "elder" opinion and am grateful for it.

Older and younger gay men are deeply suspicious of one another. Older men fear younger men just want "daddies" to take care of them. Typically, they misinterpret a younger gay man's "neediness" and worry about being used and therefore disregard these younger men, which makes their own loneliness more acute.

Older gay men tell me about being unwanted, and hold ageism accountable for how they're treated. One client told me he feels that younger gay men look right through him. Men in general prize youth and beauty in their partners. Most likely, in a sexual situation, those younger men *are* looking through him.

Nevertheless, I tell older clients who wish to mentor, befriend, or date younger gay men to keep themselves out there—available and visible. Lots of younger men want and need the advice, strength, and friendship of a gay elder. And they may want to date and have a relationship.

Many younger gay men are lonely, long for male recognition, and sometimes use sexuality to get their elders' attention. Again, this is a result of our community's not having a built-in mentor system.

One client in his 20s told me he enjoyed talking to older gays but felt awkward nonetheless. He tried to keep a distance—even when he wanted to get to know them better—because they usually interpreted his friendliness as an interest in sex. Both of these types of men lose out!

In mentoring, trust is essential, but trust is rare in the gay community. Trust of other men is low among men in general. Many straight women I know talk about not trusting the men who pay attention to them. Most of the attention they've received has been sexual, so they hold men suspect. Straight men usually don't have to worry about that from other men. But they do harbor a general distrust for one another, regardless of age and orientation.

Reparative therapies teach that a man struggling with unwanted gay desires is a man who wasn't mentored. As a boy, he wasn't man enough—he didn't live up to the masculine ideal. The only men who could guide him appropriately were straight. But even straight men lack appropriate mentoring! Most initiations into manhood are through sports, religion, and dating girls. If none of that's part of your life, male culture pushes you aside and abandons you. This is true for gays and straights alike.

A lot of straight men I treat didn't get blessings from their fathers or other men in their lives. They feel deeply wounded and starved for affirmations. They are not gay or bi-attractional—they just need healthy role models. Through therapy, I become a mentor for them or help them find other men in their lives to help make them stronger.

The same is true for gay men, only more so. In his popular and widely respected book *Being Homosexual: Gay Men and Their Development,* Richard Isay states: "If the fathers of homosexual boys were accepting and loving toward them, these children would have a model for loving and caring for other men, a model that has not been traditionally available in our society. Fathers who nurture the development of their homosexual sons, who affirm their worth by giving their time and attention, encouraging and supporting their son's interests, and who are not dismissive or censorious, will help their sons to be capable, as gay adults, of loving, affectionate, and sexually responsive lasting relationships."[3] I believe Isay speaks for all men—gay, bi-attractional, and straight. If all fathers demonstrated the role model that Isay discusses, heterosexual men could have trusting, solid, and supportive relationships with other men. Gay and bi-attractional men could have the same, along with healthy sexual/romantic relationships.

We also need to be mentored in adult love relationships. Richard Isay affirms, "Gay men also long to satisfy a desire for closeness to their father that has so often been thwarted or frustrated in childhood. This longing is obvious in the young man looking for an older partner, but it is also seen in the older man who treats his youthful lover with kindness and care and, identifying with him, gets the love that he longs for himself."[4]

This phenomenon mirrors heterosexual men and women who try to meet their emotional needs through older and younger partners. It is unrelated to sexual and romantic orientation, but finds its roots in unmet needs from childhood. Clearly, relationships are a way to heal and work through those early needs—as you'll see in the last three chapters of this book.

Also important is the need to be mentored by witnessing other successful gay relationships. For my partner and me, it's been extremely nourishing to be close friends with a number of other gay male couples. Watching heterosexual couples can also offer insights into standard relationship strategies such as anger management, conflict resolution, and open communication (to name just a few!).

Straight partners must address their gender differences. Gay men must address the unique things about a male-male relationship: sexual gratification, competitiveness, empathy skills, and other challenging social and genetic traits. The only way to get that form of mentoring is either from another male couple or from a man who's been in healthy gay relationships.

HIV has stolen many of our gay elders. Before the latest drugs, so many gay men died, leaving the younger ones alone. While AIDS has been horrible and devastating, it has also forced out of the closet many men who may never have come out otherwise. A terminal diagnosis is a profound existential experience.

Reflecting on life, you start to recognize what really matters. In the '80s, men languishing in hospitals started to talk about being gay and wanted their partners by their side. Gay men took the risk of writing about being gay, and news cameras began entering gay households. This was the only positive part of AIDS. We could finally say, "There is a brave gay man." We all stand on the shoulders of those men who, toward the end of their lives, decided it was important to stand up and speak.

My suggestions for finding a mentor:

1. Overcome your anxieties and speak directly to a gay man you admire. He can be chronologically older, or in a more mature place in his gay life. Let him know that you appreciate where he is in his life and that you would like to talk to him about what has worked and what hasn't. "You seem on the ball and I enjoy hearing your stories about your life as a gay man. Would you be willing to go to coffee and share more?"

2. If a man comes on to you and you aren't interested, tell him. This can be done in a polite, respectful way. Let him know you enjoy his company, but you aren't interested in a romantic and sexual relationship. To honor his feelings, you can ask him, "Will that work for you?"

My suggestions for older men who want to mentor:

1. Don't stay away from certain gay events just because you think you are "too old." Yes, some men there will think you are, but there'll also be men who'll be glad to see you. Remember that many younger gay men are starved for role models and mature relationships.

2. If you see a young man you'd like to get to know, tell him you think he has a lot going for him and you would like to get to know him better. If he seems apprehensive, let him know you are not interested in being sexual with him and that you are genuinely interested in him as a person. If he doesn't believe you and nothing comes of it, don't take it personally. This isn't about you. You've continued to pave the road for yourself by offering the possibility of a mentoring friendship. You might have negative feelings about the rejection—that is normal. Healthy self-talk might be, "That man has his own reasons for not wanting advice and counsel from me. This isn't about me as a gay man or as a person."

3. Go to your local gay community center and let them know you want to be a gay elder and/or gay mentor. If they don't have a program like this available, tell them you'd like to start one.

In *Golden Men: The Power of Gay Midlife,* Harold Kooden and Charles Flowers write, "Our middle years will become golden only if we treat ourselves as if we were carved from real gold: precious, sexy, infinitely malleable, and priceless."[5] I want midlife elders to adopt this attitude. Go into the gay community and see yourself as the priceless asset you are.

References

1. John R. Stowe, *Gay Spirit Warrior: An Empowerment Workbook for Men Who Love Men.* Tallahassee, FL: Findhorn Press (1999).

2. Erik Erikson, *Childhood and Society.* New York: W.W. Norton and Company (1963).

3. Richard Isay, *Being Homosexual: Gay Men and Their Development.* Northvale, NJ: Jason Aronson (1994).

4. Richard Isay, *Becoming Gay: The Journey to Self-Acceptance.* New York: Pantheon Books (1996).

5. Harold Kooden with Charles Flowers, *Golden Men: The Power of Gay Midlife.* New York: Avon Books (2000).

Chapter 7
Take Advantage of Therapy "Workouts"

WE SEE THE WORLD AS WE ARE, NOT AS IT IS.
—the Talmud

Not long ago, homosexuality was viewed as a mental disorder. In 1973 it was finally removed from the second edition of the *Diagnostic and Statistical Manual of Mental Disorders* (known, for short, as *DSM II*).

You'll recall that as a 15-year-old in 1978, I sat with a therapist who strongly believed that homosexual tendencies resulted from a dominant, smothering mother and a distant, mostly absent father. While my therapist helped me in many ways, we always argued about whether I was gay. He believed it wasn't my true orientation. I knew it was—and that I could not change, try as I might. To me, however, he was a "doctor," an authority figure. So I tried dating a girl named Laurie. While she taught me to French kiss, I fantasized that she was Billy, the boy in class whom I was in love with. I told my therapist that girls did nothing for me and that I was drawn to boys. He asked me for details of my sexual and romantic interest in boys, and I talked to him about it—twice a week, for three years. He helped me with my teenage struggles and also encouraged me to be open and frank about my homosexuality, and for that I'm grateful. Without his insistence that I talk candidly about my homosexuality and my determination to get what I wanted out of life, I couldn't have come out at the young that I did, much less start a practice for mostly gay and lesbian clients.

In 1980, in the *DSM*'s third edition, the term *ego-dystonic* homosexuality was created to describe the person who was uncomfortable, or in conflict, with his homosexuality and who wanted to change his orientation. Typically, he'd report either that homosexual urges interfered with his life or that his lack of heterosexual arousal hindered the lifestyle he desired. The opposite term, *ego-syntonic* homosexuality, was used to acknowledge the significant number of gays and lesbians who were quite satisfied with their sexual and romantic orientation and showed no signs of psychopathology.

Ego-dystonic homosexuality remained in the *DSM III* until 1987, when the manual was revised as *DSM III-R.* The board concluded that *all* gays and lesbians start out as ego-dystonic (that is, uncomfortable with their orientation). Upon fully coming out, they become ego-syntonic and comfortable with being gay. (But you already know this, after reading Chapter 2!)

The present *DSM-IV* doesn't include homosexuality as a disorder, but still permits a diagnosis of "Sexual Disorder, Not Otherwise Specified" for anyone with "persistent and marked distress about sexual orientation"—the same diagnosis used for sexual addiction and compulsivity.[1] (There is talk of creating a diagnostic category of sexual addiction for the next edition of the *DSM,* but as of this writing it does not exist.)

Unfortunately, thousands of gay men harbor misgivings about entering therapy; they fear hiring a therapist who won't be objective. Many of them seek gay or lesbian therapists, but this isn't necessarily the best step. A gay therapist offers no guarantee that you won't still receive doses of homophobia and heterosexism. "Homonegativity" is a lesser form of homophobia. The gay or lesbian person may feel good about being gay but still cultivate negative thoughts about gay culture in general.

I use the Gay and Lesbian Affirmative Psychotherapeutic approach, which addresses the severe psychological consequences of homophobia and heterosexism. It stresses that the problem isn't with the gay individual but with what's been done *to* that person. When a gay man comes out of the closet, he loses many of the privileges heterosexual males take for granted—and his grief over this loss is often profound.

Dan, a 32-year-old single man, heard that I specialize in sexual addiction and came to me for help for what he called "sexually compulsive behaviors." He was soft-spoken, with a strong tendency toward passivity. He simply responded to events in life rather than taking charge of his own destiny. He was an active member of a church-related organization that focused on "healing homosexuality." The behaviors he referred to were "relapses" during which he would masturbate to "homosexual" fantasies. (I'm putting "homosexual" in quotes because he used this adjective in a pejorative way.)

During our evaluation appointment, he told me he was an "ex-gay man" and that he wanted to stay that way. Dan also admitted that he had no sexual interest in women. All his sexual and romantic urges were directed toward adult males. His life goal was to become a celibate monk in the Roman Catholic Church. Thus, any masturbation was deeply troubling to him, and his "slips" caused him depression. He described gay men as "homosexuals," followers of the "alternative lifestyle." He thought that his own homosexual urges were the result of poor, inappropriate fathering.

As we learned in earlier chapters, these are the teachings of "reparative therapies" such as the one Don attended through his church. I told him I was gay and—given how he felt about homosexuality—that he should be aware of my disagreement with his views should we enter into a therapeutic relationship.

To my surprise, he said that wouldn't bother him. He didn't feel my beliefs would interfere with my ability to help his "sexually compulsive behaviors." He did want assurance that I wouldn't try to convince him that being gay was the answer to his problems. I did assure him I wouldn't try to convince him to be gay—my job is to help clients identify what's right for them. But to be honest, I told him that most likely, his "masturbatory slips with homosexual imagery" resulted from his attempts to suppress something natural to him. Dan didn't agree with this, but he remained eager to begin the therapeutic process.

In my office I keep a photograph of my partner, Mike, and me, along with pictures of my young nephews, my sister, and my brother-in-law. Dan asked, "Are you happy with your partner?" I answered, "Yes, very happy." He doubted that any gay man could be happy in an "incomplete" partnership lacking the "complementary female element" (in the words of his reparative therapy group).

I encouraged Dan to talk more about how he felt about me—and my being gay—thus inviting the process of transference, which I explained in Chapter 1. Dan had already begun transferring his negative feelings about his own homosexuality onto me. This was a positive sign that his therapy had let him understand himself more. During our sessions, he referred to homosexuality as a "sad lifestyle." He thought I was not truly happy, that I had convinced myself otherwise, and that I was "giving in" to my homosexual urges. He stayed in therapy for approximately eight months, then cancelled an appointment and never returned.

If Dan was gay, he couldn't come to terms with it, for his own personal and religious reasons. I respected his decision to refrain from acting on his homosexual urges, because that's what he wanted to do. But I did question his efforts to deny them and "repair" them. That struggle caused him more depression and difficulty than if he'd just accepted that he was a gay man who'd vowed to live a celibate life.

Keeping one's urges "dirty" and taboo only makes them stronger. When Dan said I was giving in to my homosexuality—something not in my best interest—he was projecting his struggle onto me. In reality, Dan was fooling himself to think he could suppress his own homosexual urges; in fact, *he* was "giving in": to religion and antigay therapies that said there was something wrong with him.

Most religious institutions spurn gay men. Rejected by their clergy, ostracized and outcast from their house of worship, religious gay men often replace religion with therapy. I've had many gay Catholic clients who probably would never have come to me if they could have gone to a priest for support and assistance, and if their church had accepted their gayness. No matter what issue they present, I often find they're really looking for spiritual direction and insight—not something I'm equipped to provide—and they become frustrated.

In my practice I've met gay men who called themselves "recovering Catholics." They spent years in therapy, trying to undo the damage of hearing, throughout their lives, that gay sex is an "abomination" and that they'll go to hell if they "practice" it.

In my groups, I always tell the men, "A new member will be starting next week." That's all I say. Father Arturo, as I'll call him, entered the group, admitted he was sexually active, and said he needed to talk about being gay—then identified himself as a priest. The group (85% Catholic) had a very negative reaction. One member told me I should have "warned" them Father Arturo was coming so they could prepare themselves or leave before he arrived. I wasn't aware of the strong judgment that many gay Catholic men hold against priests, and I simply wasn't prepared for how they would respond to a sexually active one.

While growing up, these men felt wounded by priests. Father Arturo was the lightning rod for all of their anger and sorrow. But he was up for the challenge! He raised all sorts of new issues—which everyone could work on and explore more fully. It became a therapeutic opportunity, not just for the group, but for Father Arturo. Through these other men's judgments, he was forced to work through his own issues about being gay and sexually active.

I joke that I'm glad to be Jewish, because much of what I learned in Hebrew school was conducted primarily in that language. If the rabbi fulminated against homosexuality as a sin and an abomination, I didn't understand a word he said. This always gets a laugh!

As we know, children are taught not to act, feel, or think in certain ways, and not to experience all their bodily sensations. At various workshops I've conducted, gay men have itemized the various "don'ts" they received as boys:

"Don't act like a sissy."
"Don't be a crybaby."
"Don't touch yourself down there."
"Don't aspire to be a ballet dancer, artist, musician, or actor."

"Don't sit with your legs crossed."

"Don't shake hands like a limp fish."

"Don't look at or touch other boys, and don't let them touch you."

These admonitions are all inherently sexist. If there's anything "feminine" about a boy, our social conventions lead us to believe there must be something wrong with him. Implicit in these elements of our culture is the message that there's something wrong with females! Yet we don't restrict girls in the same way. It's fine for them to play sports or to wear a suit and a tie to work. Girls are allowed to touch one another's hair and bodies, hug one another, and even go to the bathroom together.

I think this is why young gay men become aware of their orientation earlier than lesbians do: When we want to touch other boys or feel drawn to play with "girl things," we quickly realize we're different. Not until later do girls discover it's "wrong" to enjoy physical intimacy with other females.

One of my clients was told, "Men shouldn't be vulnerable." Another was warned, "Don't let others know your business." Boys who accept these messages find it hard to let others into their lives and to be open about their vulnerability. This problem isn't specific to gay men; everyone has to grapple with repressive social messages.

Erik Erikson described the stages of physical, emotional, and psychological development and assigned specific developmental issues—or tasks, as he called them—to each psychosocial stage. He believed that if any stage was vandalized or interrupted, the child would suffer throughout his adult life until he resolved his wounding from that stage.

Erikson is still widely read for his clear insights into psychological dynamics, which even lay readers can appreciate. In *The Life Cycle Completed*,[2] he investigates each of these psychological stages. I'll cover just the ones most pertinent to gay men.

The play-age child or, as we would call him today, the preschooler (age 2-6), begins to *initiate* games and pretend stories, not just imitate others on the playground. At this stage, he develops a sense of right and wrong and starts to develop a sense of purpose and identity by dressing up in adult clothes and playing with dolls and action figures, trucks and cranes, and other goal-oriented toys.

At this stage, gay boys suffer early wounding and other negative influences. Once a gay boy in his preschool years starts to display an affinity for feminine toys, his father often distances himself from his "sissy" son. He might even be critical and shaming. In *The "Sissy Boy Syndrome" and the Development of Homosexuality,* Richard Green reports a study in which 75% of the boys who played with female toys and identified with girls grew up to be gay.[3] Girl-play doesn't *make* a boy gay, but it's one of the early indicators that he is. Also, not all gay boys play with girls' toys—which indicates that their wounding might not have occurred at this stage.

We expect a good father to interact with his children, but because boys aren't supposed to play with dolls, they are rarely allowed time to "practice" with them as a child. When my first nephew was born and my sister let me hold him or change his diaper, I had no idea what I was doing. Having not been allowed to play with dolls, I was never conditioned to know what to do.

I can't tell you how many gay men and lesbians—at my workshops, in group therapy, and in individual therapy in my office—have cried over memories of being told that wanting to play like the opposite gender was wrong. Obviously this kind of shame can have effects that last into adulthood.

If a young boy's caregivers encourage him at this stage, he'll learn that certain things are allowed or not allowed—but without feeling shame or guilt. Gay little boys then feel free to use their imaginations and engage in make-believe and role-playing without having to hide.

During a boy's school-age years (approximately 6-12), he must develop competence and a sense of achievement by completing tasks and following directions. He develops a sense of self-worth.

Here, caregivers and teachers must afford the child intellectual stimulation and help him to acquire skills that will enable him to be productive and successful. If children don't develop a sense of competence, they instead form a sense of inferiority. As adults, such children can become obsessively competitive with others. In my practice—and in the gay community in general—I see lots of insecure people with strong tendencies to compete. They have to "keep up with the Joneses" to feel good about themselves. Many of them feel threatened by other gay men's successes, relationships, and social and monetary status.

This particular neurosis is a conditioned trait in American culture, but for gay men I believe it's more than that. Most gay boys get grief because they throw a ball like a girl, sit like a girl, can't fight, and don't fit in groups with other boys because they're different. They begin to feel totally incompetent as men. This is a huge issue that we explore in workshops: Our masculinity has been wounded as a result of the many negative messages we've received.

For the most part, heterosexual men find sports to be a good outlet for healthy (and sometimes unhealthy) competition. But we gay men tend to go to a gym rather than join a team. As a result, there's a lot of unhealthy competing over looks, muscles, and endowment.

Perhaps our worst wounds occur during adolescence, between ages 12 and 18. Here is where all the earlier stages become integrated. Does the young man display a strong sense of independence, a basic sense of trust, and strong feelings of competence? Does he feel in control of his life? According to Erikson, adolescence is the most crucial stage. If the individual can manage this crisis successfully by integrating all the stages in a healthy way, he'll be ready to head out into the world and ready to plan for his future. If not, however, the teen will feel incompetent, have difficulty making decisions, and remain confused about his sexual orientation, future career, and his role in life in general. In addition to the normal pitfalls that Erikson talks about, gay and lesbian adolescents have additional challenges. Gay and lesbian teens are confused about their sexual identity, largely because they're not allowed to explore it in a healthy, productive way.

During this period of "identity crisis," a teen develops his authentic self. To figure out who he really is, he hangs out with peer groups, who give him a sense of belonging. He tries to assemble a coherent self-image from an array of many different roles: jock, leather-jacketed rebel, SAT scholar, computer geek, "most popular" or "most likely to succeed," or just all-around good guy.

A gay teenager is robbed of his sense of belonging. The kid who seems to be gay—even if he isn't—is the one everyone wants to avoid. He has to play at heterosexuality, date girls, and pretend to be someone he's not. The negative impact is profound.

Erickson refers to the next developmental stage as the young adult years (age 19-40). Here the choice is between personal commitment to another human being (in the role of partner, spouse, or parent) and isolation. The young man learns about sex, love, and intimacy—the latter, to my mind, the most important of the three. The task is to integrate sex with romance and infatuation.

Now love relationships become central. Erikson believed that no matter how successful a man is, he's not developmentally complete without intimacy. If all goes well, the young adult bonds with others and enjoys a secure sense of identity. If not, he'll fear commitment and find it difficult to depend on anyone. Many gay men find themselves isolated because homophobia and heterosexism have kept them from developing intimacy skills.

Individual and group psychotherapy can help gay men work through unresolved issues in adolescence and young adulthood. For the adolescent, peer groups become an extremely important influence. At school, he'll develop a stronger sense of self, become separate from—which isn't to say rebellious against—his parents, and feel a sense of belonging.

During the next stage—young adulthood—we start role-playing at heterosexuality. In an episode of the sitcom *Will and Grace*, Will's acting teacher asks whether Will has any acting experience. He tells her that he acted as a straight man for about 19 years. She responds, "Not very well, I imagine!" Funny as that may be, it's sad that a young man should have to pretend to be anything other than who he really is.

In his book *Now That I'm Out, What Do I Do?* Brian McNaught writes that most gay men "have been enormously, if not consciously, traumatized by the social pressure they felt to identify and behave as…heterosexual, even though such pressure is not classified as sexual abuse by experts in the field. Imagine how today's society would respond if heterosexual 13- to 19-year-olds were forced to date someone of the same sex. What would the reaction be if they were expected to hold the hand of, slow dance with, hug, kiss and say, 'I love you' to someone to whom they were not…sexually attracted? The public would be outraged! Adult supervisors would be sent to prison. Youthful 'perpetrators' would be expelled from school. Years of therapy would be prescribed for the innocent victims of such abuse… Yet that's part of the everyday life of gay teenagers."[4]

That's why the type of therapy I offer gay men is similar, in many ways, to what's provided for clients who were sexually abused in childhood. If they suffered the kind of covert *cultural* sexual abuse we discussed earlier, therapy needs to address that particular experience.

Some therapists simply present themselves as a blank screen, showing little or no emotion ("flat affect," the term is) and providing minimum feedback. They do not share anything about themselves with the client. In effect, they hope to hold up a mirror for their clients to offer them an opportunity to examine their own projections. This type of therapy has its place, but because the typical gay man entering therapy has a long history of emotional (and romantic) disconnections, this approach isn't usually effective.

For a sexual abuse survivor, the "blank screen" approach is ineffective for the same reasons. The world in which he lives is already a blank screen; the heterosexual culture's lack of response to a gay man's suffering is a primary cause of his psychological distress. His therapist keeping him at emotional arm's length only buttresses his original frustration when he found himself unable to connect to society at large. To heal a gay man who feels isolated and alone, safety and trust are essential within the therapeutic relationship. It's no help to sit with him and simply nod without offering feedback to help him transform his experience through dialogue.

Individual therapy can help heal the wounds a gay child sustains when his early attempts to learn attachment skills are frustrated. If his mother *was* overly protective (attached) and if his father was overly detached, the young gay child learns to expect love either from a distance or overly close—"enmeshed," as psychologists call it. Thus, as an adult, he might either keep too much distance between himself and friends and partners, or tend to get too close.

I try to help gay men learn that love is a balance of togetherness and separateness and that going too far in either direction isn't healthy. The therapeutic relationship serves as a model for that. We establish healthy boundaries while cultivating a feeling of closeness and healthy dependency.

In individual therapy, as we've learned, the client projects or transfers onto the therapist the traits of his early childhood caretakers. Positive transference is when positive attributes are transferred onto the therapist; negative transference is when negative attributes are transferred. This also happens with our coworkers and friends—and particularly our partners, as you'll see in Chapter 9. The more emotionally close you are to someone, the more the transference will emerge.

In therapy, however, we invite transference and talk about it. The client *should* transfer those negative feelings and images onto a therapist, which enables him to travel back in time to when he was a child and experience them again—only this time with a better outcome. Now, with adult intelligence and maturity—and a therapist's help—the client is able to associate his feelings with a positive experience, thereby healing old wounds.

Positive and negative transference is especially important in dealing with gay issues. Clients who start work with me have a wide spectrum of feelings about my being an openly gay therapist. Some come wanting at least some of the life I enjoy: partnered, successful in business, and as out as can be. They enter therapy on a high because they believe I can help them get where they want to be. They idealize me, thus positively transferring onto me all the things they want. However, after a few sessions or even a few months, they begin to recognize that it took me years of work to become comfortable with myself as a gay man. They don't anticipate the effort involved.

And so the negative transference begins! Some clients become angry and say things like "You can't help me" or "I can't have what you have." Either they drop out of therapy or, if they continue, they blame me for causing them "too much pain." In time they realize that their own blocks are the only things standing in their way. It may be that they had a parent who neglected them and did not offer adequate guidance—or any guidance for that matter—particularly around being gay. As clients feel more dependent in therapy, the therapeutic relationship will more closely resemble the dependent relationships of their childhood. I become a stand-in for that neglectful parent.

This is a natural, positive indicator that a client's psychological work has begun. He begins to appreciate the struggle involved in becoming a self-actualized, self-affirming gay man. If he steps up to this challenge, he enters his *own* therapy.

As you'll see in Chapters 9 and 10, negative transference is a major stumbling block for gay men in our intimate adult relationships because as boys and young adults, few of us enjoyed positive, nonsexualized interaction with other gay men. If clients can understand that their current feelings are about their pasts, dismiss them as "ancient history," and work them out with me, they'll be primed for healthy adult love relationships.

For a gay man, entering a therapeutic relationship with an openly gay therapist is often very challenging. It may be the first time he's looked at himself and another gay man in an authentic way or talked to another gay male outside of a dark bar with loud music and alcohol. Ironically, another gay man inviting him into a healthy space for the first time can be very frightening because the relationship demands a level of intimacy, honesty, and authenticity he has never encountered. Just uttering the words "I might be gay" to another gay man produces anxiety.

An internal fight begins. He's violating the internal taboo that all men, gay and straight alike, have been taught: It's not OK to talk to another gay man except with scorn and contempt. The habit of avoiding other gay men surfaces, which makes the client want to run away from me. But for anyone just coming out, this experience can also be very exciting. For the first time he can safely, openly, and intimately explore his own orientation.

Anyone who's been out for a while and involved in the gay community has already formed ideas of what it is to be gay. If I challenge his thinking or offer him new insights, he may argue that I'm pushing an idea that doesn't jibe with his experience. My job isn't to tell a client who to be but simply to share with him the things I perceive. Even a gay man who's been out for a while may not see his own subtle forms of internalized homophobia.

John had been out for more than 20 years, but in my work with him I soon discovered he had a limited awareness of most aspects of gay life. For the past decade, being out for John had meant going to the bars exclusively, so bar life was all he knew. Now that he was in his 40s, he felt that gay men were rejecting him, which he attributed to gay culture's premium on youth. As we know, men in general can be that way and, yes, a lot of gay men only seek younger men. There are also countless men whose interests aren't so narrow and who don't go to bars. John simply hadn't run into them.

He didn't believe me when I told him the gay world was bigger than he imagined, but he wanted to, so he kept on with therapy. Through our work together, he gathered the courage to attend Gay Pride events, where he found men who were interested in him. He happily admitted that he needed to expand his notions of what gay life was all about!

Therapy offers a safe place for a client to increase his self-awareness. As transference develops, it's normal for him to bypass (consciously or not) the work he thought he came into therapy to do. Little does he know this shift in priorities *is* his work! The client will say to me, "You're comfortable with being gay only because you have a relationship," or, "Yeah, if I were successful like you, I could afford to be out and open too." What he doesn't know is that before I met Mike and my career took off, I was just as out and open as I am now. But again, this resistance is a positive indication that a client has begun his therapy. Those are *his* judgments and *his* projections—they are windows into who he is. Clues that let me get to know him better and help him get to know himself.

Sometimes my being gay elicits intense homophobia from a client. I become a container for all his rage and frustration. Some therapists are so uncomfortable with the anger that arises from negative transference that they won't explore these projections. Either they find they can't help the client, or they find other less confrontational ways to do so. But I strongly believe in letting these feelings emerge. I'm the lightening rod for the client, a stand-in for whomever he *really* needs to be angry with. The negative transference is coded information about the client.

The purpose of decoding negative transference isn't to find someone to blame. It's about identifying at whom the anger is really directed. The client can direct it toward me and talk about his anger to discover its true source. It's often unhelpful for clients to confront the actual perpetrators to "clear the air." It's safer—and usually more effective—to bring out what's been suppressed within the safe space of therapy and to work it out there. If a client needs to go to the people who originally hurt him, that's his choice. It is a choice I often support and find can be helpful. But he should first work out his problems for himself.

I often refer to the old mental tapes that we all carry with us. They begin to play as soon as we encounter difficult situations. If our current situation aligns with what we were taught, then our tapes "match up" with reality and cause no problems. But if reality contradicts what we were taught, the tapes cause conflict. Obviously, changing our tapes is easier than trying to alter—or worse, deny—reality.

In therapy, of course, every known homophobic tape is activated. In a twist on the old joke: I become the very man your parents warned you against.

As a therapist, I believe I'm hired not only to be supportive and hold open an affectionate space for a client but also to be challenging and controversial. I don't fight with clients or cause them any unnecessary pain, but I do point out occasions when something they say works against the inner and outer goals they've said they want to achieve.

In the next chapter, you'll see how partners seek "escape routes" when a relationship gets too intense and their partner gets too close. The same holds true in therapy. When a gay man starts feeling too close to me or we get too near an issue, I notice he'll react in one or more of the following ways:

1. Drop out of therapy.
2. Decide to see another therapist.
3. Rely on defenses like avoidance and resistance within therapy.

These exits are typical of many people in therapy, but with gay men I see them more often. When clients resort to these exit strategies, I try to push them, gently and compassionately, to stay with and move through their pain. I'm like the guy who spots you in the gym to help you lift that heavier weight when you're not yet strong enough to do it alone.

Gay clients often find it hard to "stick" with their pain. Moreover, a gay male therapist can make the client wonder, "Am I getting too close to this guy?" even if he knows that any good therapist has numerous boundaries in place. This is where issues of attachment, competence, and intimacy all surface, for the client as well as for me. Revisiting even the happiest childhood can be a perilous journey, and some clients try to salve their own fear by drawing me out. They do this by trying to get into my personal life by asking questions about me, putting the focus on me. By not exposing the private aspects of my life I keep the boundaries safe for the client. But being open about some aspects of my life can be very helpful. It can also help them decide my life is *not* the way they want to live. What's important is that clients have some positive images of what gay life is all about.

Transference toward me is only one way clients express negative feelings about gay life. Many complain about effeminate gays and drag queens. This internalized homophobia can only damage their self-esteem and future attempts at friendships in the gay community.

In therapy, some clients speak contemptuously about "gay ghettos." They insist we shouldn't separate ourselves from our straight counterparts. I ask, "Do you have the same feelings about Jewish neighborhoods, Little Italy, or Chinatown, where other minorities have settled in?" Their usual answer is, "Uh, no."

Jeff, 39, was the top executive at a high-powered advertising agency. Three years earlier he'd divorced his wife of 15 years to live with a male partner. He came to me because he was troubled by his sexual acting-out behavior outside of his relationship.

In our first session, Jeff said, "I'm sure you and your partner aren't monogamous. Both of you must sleep around on the other. That's just how gay life is! So how can you help me be monogamous and fit heterosexual standards onto my relationship?" Of course, Jeff was simply projecting.

He talked about going to a party where he turned around to see his partner French-kissing another guy. He said I'd understand "because that must happen at parties that you attend." He insisted that I couldn't appreciate many aspects of his situation because he'd been married to a woman and I hadn't. Another time he began to weep because he felt I'd judged him for wanting to share a life with his partner that mirrored his notion of a heterosexual ideal.

Once I'd taught him about transference, both positive and negative, and the concept of projections, Jeff's therapy workout began in earnest and he was able to find his own answers. We sorted through his various statements and used them as clues to help him discover who he was.

Right off, I told him that I did believe in monogamy. Was that Jeff's vision of what a relationship should be? I'd support it! I told him I'd be horrified to see my partner French-kissing another man. That wasn't acceptable for us, it did *not* happen at any of the parties we attended. He thought I supported promiscuity because I was gay. That, I explained, was *his* homophobic projection.

Truth is, gay men are divided on monogamy. We just talk more openly about it than straight couples. (More about this in Chapter 10.) Yes, some segments of gay culture accept open relationships, but others don't. I assured Jeff that he could find gay friends who were either monogamous or who at least respected his and his partner's boundaries.

I agreed with Jeff: I don't know all the nuances of heterosexual marriage. But I've treated hundreds of men who were married, and I was open to learning more. Jeff's fear that he couldn't be understood was another instance of transference. During his marriage, he believed that if he told people his real feelings, no one would understand. This problem went back to his childhood. When little Jeffrey tried to talk about a problem, his parents wouldn't give him any time or attention, and he felt misunderstood. Now he was projecting these old feelings onto me.

Jeff understood that much of what he saw in gay life reflected his own limited awareness about being gay. He was able to identify his negative transference toward me as his resentment toward his parents (as well as other gay men who'd harshly judged him for wanting to apply heterosexual standards to his relationship with his partner). He wanted to be conservative, monogamous, and have a stable circle of friends. To move in that direction, he went through lots of tears, anger, sadness, and joy.

It's OK to argue. Let differences exist! If my opinions don't work for a client, sometimes he'll say, "Joe, that works for you, but not for me." I accept that.

Therapy is about owning—and taking charge of—your own thoughts, judgments, feelings, transference, and projections. This means tracking them back to the source to examine what they tell you about yourself.

A heterosexual therapist offers gay men other types of beneficial transference challenges. The client may worry that his therapist will try to make him straight (as his parents may have done)—or he may even hope he'll be successful in doing so! The straight male therapist can also stand in for society as a whole or represent the heterosexual privileges that a gay man will lose by coming out. Working with a straight therapist who is willing to tackle these issues can be very rewarding and healing.

"Group therapy" also benefits gay men by imparting a sense of belonging and helping them to develop social skills they never had a chance to practice in childhood. This can be a client's first time around a group of other gay men in a setting with lights on and no chemicals or sex involved. In my very first group session that I ran, every gay man was tense, anxious, and nervous, including myself. It was new terrain for all of us!

Whatever a man's doing out in the real world, for good or ill he'll bring it with him into group therapy. Once clients enter group therapy, I see how they relate to others and how others relate to them—live, unplugged, and uncensored. I can intervene, interpret, and give feedback on the spot so that their future encounters can have healthier outcomes.

Your first group was the family that shaped you. Inevitably, someone in group therapy will remind you of your mother, father, brother, or sister. These similarities offer many opportunities for reparative and corrective experiences as you re-experience that (pleasantly or unpleasantly) familiar energy—this time with a different outcome.

Your second group was the one that helped you learn to socialize. Again, someone here will remind you of an old friend, boss, bully, neighbor, rabbi, priest, ex-partner, or someone who was important in the years you ventured away from your family into the schools and churches you attended. Again, opportunities arise for some healing work to be done with these "stand-ins" in group.

Getting men to both enter and participate in a gay men's group is a challenge! The first thing I almost always hear is "I don't want to sit in a room full of queens feeling like victims and bitching about their lives." I reply that the group isn't like that at all—griping and whining aren't allowed. Either men come around to do their work or they leave.

Some say they want feedback from a professional like me, but not from other "screwed-up" people. I point out that these group members are their peers, not authority figures. All too often, individual therapy is a one-sided relationship where the client speaks only about himself, and there's a limit to what I can contribute—in terms of my own personal insights and struggles—so that the experience stays therapeutic. A gay men's group is more like the real world. To get to the core of who he is, each man shares his personal struggles and needs to hear—and react to—the judgments of other laymen. I'm on hand to step in if someone offers inappropriate or unhelpful feedback.

Which isn't to say group sessions aren't sometimes rough-and-tumble. You want to hear even misguided judgments and reactions because these challenges to your self-representation will prepare you for what you regularly encounter "out there" in real life.

Transference and projection arise in group just as in individual therapy. As I mentioned earlier, one member may remind another of a relative or past partner. Another man may have a bad reaction to another group member or even develop romantic feelings for him. This lively interaction provides a rich opportunity for insight, growth, and healing. This is why a combination of group and individual therapy is ideal. Gay clients can work out their intimacy issues privately, then bring what they've learned to their group.

Whenever a member voices frustration about how the group is operating, others usually join in. This is typical behavior as the men learn how to empower themselves. In a gay men's group with a gay therapist, however, I've found the "complaint chorus" is more forceful and bullying then in a mixed group. But this important acting-out allows more family dynamics to arise. How were you treated while growing up within your family? What's it like to have the support of other group members (your siblings) lobbying against Dad (the therapist)? How were you treated as a gay male? Exploring these issues can help heal childhood wounds.

To ensure emotional and physical safety, I enforce a few non-negotiable guidelines. The most important of these is confidentiality. Any gay community is small enough that group members might have friends in common. Therefore, respecting every man's confidence is imperative, during group and in all the years following, so that no one needs to worry about being "outed" as having attended group therapy.

No group member is allowed to be sexual, date, or even socialize with any other member. There are strong reasons for this. First,
the group is where *all* the work needs to be done. Problems can arise
if outside sub-groups or friendships develop. One man may innocently tell another something he doesn't want mentioned in front of
the others. This erodes the principle that all admissions must stay
within the confines of the group. Having to keep secrets drove men
to enter group therapy in the first place, and private "sharings" tend
to dilute the group's energy and overall purpose.

Only the chemical-free may attend. If a participant is taking prescribed medications, fine. But if he's had even one drink with dinner, I ask him to leave. One group member confided that he was
high on marijuana. He argued that if he stated the truth, he deserved
to stay. A good example of negative transference! He wasn't willing
to look at his drug problem, so he blamed both me and the group
when I asked him to leave. He had broken the agreed-upon group
contract of not using nonprescribed drugs and was not willing to
take responsibility for that.

The group triggers feelings and runs on emotion; anyone who
suppresses them with nonprescribed drugs or alcohol is hindering
our collective effort. Therapy can't work if someone's mood and
mind are altered. Moreover, some members are in recovery. It just
makes sense to keep group sessions drug-free.

Group is all about forging and exploring relationships with other
gay men. You'll get support from others, but you must be there for
them as well. Given our strong hardwiring *not* to be there for other
gay men, this is sometimes difficult. When you're single it's so much
easier! You can pick and choose the experiences you want, deciding
exactly how much—or how little—energy you want to devote to
them. This is also true for individual therapy: It's up to you how
much you want to share, at your own pace. But in group, just as with
a partner, the need for cooperation figures into the equation. We
meet each week. No matter what your expectations, you have to be
there on time and ready to go wherever the process takes us all.

For a few weeks, you can choose not to share anything personal.

Just sitting and listening to others' work will trigger your own thoughts and feelings. You'll be doing work on your own, whether you know it or not.

You'll learn insights and techniques you'll need in any relationship with a partner. You can seldom predict what someone else will say or what feelings and thoughts will arise. Similarly, in relationships you don't know what your day-to-day interactions with your partner will generate. To achieve intimacy, living with—and learning from—uncertainty is a must. Any relationship pulls you into uncharted terrain, whether or not you want to go there. And that's a good thing!

In one session, Will talked about his guilt about coming out to some of his family but not to others. Mario, another group member, turned to him and said, "I'm tired of hearing that story over and over again. You need to move on."

Will was very upset. "This is supposed to be a safe place for me to talk about my feelings without judgment!"

Mario insisted that he'd meant it in a kind, loving way. He felt that Will was stuck and needed to hear that kind of feedback—and, Mario *was* tired of hearing the story.

Will was very angry and threatened to leave the group. Mario began to cry and stated that he thought this was a place where "I could express myself and not have to hold back."

Yes, the group is a safe place to let your feelings, thoughts, and story unfold. But safety doesn't mean no one will ever challenge you. It does mean no one will call you hurtful names, abandon you emotionally or physically, or disrespect your most heartfelt feelings. You deserve respect, and the other group members deserve respect from you.

Mario had every right to give Will feedback, though group process demands that Mario examine his feelings too. Other group members didn't have the same reaction. So, as any group should, we helped Mario explore what in *his* history had made him especially sensitive to Will's repeating his story.

We discovered that while Mario was growing up, his parents recycled their own hassles over and over, without ever working through the issues or trying to heal them. Their endless rehearsal of gripes made Mario frustrated and confused. Mario began to see that Will's case was different—he *needed* to recycle his story for a while to make progress and work through his guilt. Once Mario recognized where his frustration with Will was coming from, he started to move toward the issue with his parents. Will turned out to be the catalyst for this work.

Then, of course, we had to look at why Will was angry with Mario. True, many people would be have been angered by Mario's comment, but Will's loud reaction and desire to leave indicated something deeper than just his reaction to Mario.

After Will calmed down, he said he'd "heard" Mario tell him his work was wrong and that he was getting nowhere. This, of course, was the same message his own family still sent him. Whenever Will made progress, his family simply downplayed it, which made him feel "bad" and "wrong." Quite unsuspectingly, Mario had stepped into Will's long-standing resentment. Will had "heard" Mario echo the tape Will ran in his own head.

Mario was honestly interested in Will's progress, and his wanting Will to move on did come from his concern that Will not stay stuck. Indeed, in Will's family, staying stuck was actually rewarded. No one had ever challenged him to do better. So instead of seeing the care—something foreign to Will—behind Mario's remark, he felt only the hurt that accompanied his belief that he'd made yet another "bad decision."

In individual therapy, insights like Will's do occur from time to time between therapist and client. In group, however, there's a much greater likelihood that they'll happen, and happen much faster because everyone is self-disclosing. All the members of the group get insights out of their exchanges, which helps to deepen their work. Mario and Will wouldn't have perceived the issues underlying their reactions without the help of the other group members and me.

Obviously group can be very intense. Like Will and Mario, members never know what will trigger a confrontation. Again, a confrontation is a positive indicator that the group is on the right track, but it can make meetings scary to attend.

Group is about intimacy—learning what it's like to be close to other gay men. Week by week, the men get emotionally more familiar with one another. It's hard not to when they're disclosing vital, personal aspects of their lives. This is the reason for the rule that anyone planning to leave must give the group at least three weeks' notice. Most people have a hard time saying goodbye. Simply to disappear after months or years, or to call me and say "I'm done with group," dishonors the men who've shared your confidence.

On the first week of his termination, a man announces that he's leaving and explains his decision. The next week, he says goodbye to each group member and talks about how each man touched him and describes what he's taking from his experience with them all. On the last week, each man, including me, says goodbye. Other members give him feedback to let him know what they hope he'll continue to work on.

As you'll see in Chapters 9 and 10, romantic long-term relationships bring on the unexpected. If you want things to go one way, the man in your life might have other ideas. Practicing these skills—not 24/7, but only once a week—is the luxury of group.

Group helps to heal gay men's deep hurt over not being witnessed. In a perfect world, you could say how you felt to someone who was bothering you—or whom you admired and liked—and he'd hear you. But even in the gay community, others don't often want to hear our personal stories or to help us examine our lives. Group demands that others listen to your pains and joys and that you witness theirs in return.

In most books, movies, and TV shows, romances are heterosexual. To relate to these stories, we gay men must identify with the woman or imagine the "hero" as gay. Either way, we're not given valid role models.

I recall the first time I watched a movie about gay men. Seeing two men having a deep relationship, kissing in a romantic way, or even flirting with each other brought tears to my eyes. The gay community desperately needs more positive, affirming images. Group brings similar "success stories" to life, and there's no need to "translate" heterosexual experience into our gay contexts. Group members hear stories about gay men in the company of other men. Group members can picture themselves in these stories, and this therapeutic mirroring offers deep healing.

Missing a session may indicate a number of things. A member may rationalize that he's just giving himself a breather that night, but he could be missing a very important opportunity. Moreover, he sends the message that other group members aren't as important as he is, and that he doesn't feel an obligation to be there for them. As a result, I don't allow more than four absences a year. If a man cannot commit to this, he simply can't enter the group.

Commitment is a major issue for men in general and for gay men in particular. Individual therapy can be paced differently, so that the client can miss a few sessions or take breaks, but group invites a deeper level of commitment. You're creating new pathways for intimacy that will benefit you outside that group.

In a physical workout, you strain to lift weights so that when you leave the gym you're stronger, more fit, and more self-confident. Individual therapy is like having a personal trainer. But as any bodybuilder will tell you, working out where other men are also sweating and struggling is a powerful inducement to complete your full regimen. (Couples, of course, already constitute their own "group," as you'll see in Chapters 9 and 10.)

Many gay men do whatever it takes to avoid coming into therapy—like many straight people—because of the implication that they're weak and can't help themselves. This is, in part, why I give talks and hold weekend workshops. They let wary individuals attend something that doesn't have the "therapy" stigma. They can get their feet wet. They meet me and see that I'm not so scary. And when they meet other people who are in therapy, they begin to challenge their belief that therapy can't help them.

These weekend workshops also enhance what is already happening for men in therapy. While workshops are not therapy, they are *therapeutic* and can become part of their treatment. Attending workshops can speed their recovery process and offer insights that neither individual nor group therapy can offer. Just as group accelerates and deepens one's work in individual therapy, weekend workshops enhance the group therapy experience.

Gay partners who are afraid to enter therapy together can attend a "Getting the Love You Want" (GTLYW) couples workshop, become familiar with me and with the material, and see for themselves whether they might want to venture into regular therapy. For gay men in ongoing individual or group therapy, attending a GTLYW couples workshop with their partner can be extremely beneficial. I used to work with individuals for long periods and spent a lot of time helping them heal and grow. But when they went back to their partners who weren't in the therapy loop, things between them would break down. My clients had learned a new way of living that was foreign to their partners, which tended to cause some turbulence or even jeopardize the relationship.

In the GTLYW workshop, gay and lesbian couples are there together in the same room, which can be awkward at first, since in general gays and lesbians don't socialize together. But by the middle of the workshop, both sets of couples begin to feel the advantages of each other's presence and interaction. Lesbian couples offer gay male couples insights they didn't have before, and vice versa. There is no forced interaction between the couples, so that provides a level of comfort as well.

I encourage individuals I work with to do the workshop to bring their partners up to speed. They see the information their partner's absorbing and learn tools to keep communication lines open so that both of them can grow together to ensure that their relationship stays whole and strong.

References

1. *Diagnostic and Statistical Manual of Mental Disorders* (known, for short, as *DSM II*).

2. Joan M. Erikson, *The Life Cycle Completed.* New York: Norton Publishers (1997).

3. Richard Green, *The "Sissy Boy Syndrome" and the Development of Homosexuality.* New Haven: Yale University Press (1987).

4. Brian McNaught, *Now That I'm Out, What Do I Do?* New York: St. Martin's Press (1997).

Chapter 8
Maintain Rewarding Relationships

LIFE IS CHANGE. GROWTH IS OPTIONAL. CHOOSE WISELY.
—Karen Kaiser Clark

Steve, 41 years old, had been out for a long time and had tended bar at a gay club before becoming an ad salesman. He came to me after his partner of five years said "I'm leaving you."

Steve admitted that he had a negative view of gay culture. At the bar where he used to work he'd seen countless men date one another, only to break up in record time. Relationships seemed to last two months, tops.

During his 15 years as a bartender he'd struggled to find his own Mr. Right. But eventually he came to believe it simply wasn't possible. He assumed gay culture was most accessible through the bar scene, and he never considered exploring any other avenues.

Steve's eyes were warm and sensitive, which made his craggy features even more attractive. When he talked about his childhood, I saw that his parents had neglected him. They even nicknamed him Ugly—in an "endearing way," Steve said. Indeed, Steve *felt* ugly, which he attributed to a broken nose he'd suffered in a fistfight and to his aging body. In truth, Steve was a handsome guy. His distinctive nose added to the attractive ruggedness he embodied. Just over 6 feet tall and well-built, he had a pleasingly deep, resonant voice.

In high school, students had made fun of his nose. Girls didn't want to date him and called him "Z-Nose." He described himself as heavy-set and awkward. But after he'd grown thinner into his 20s and an operation had straightened his nose a bit, men in gay bars pursued him. According to Steve, the bar hired him because he was "good-looking."

Still, Steve couldn't see himself this way, so his self-esteem depended on external compliments. After becoming an ad salesman, he met Todd at the bar where he used to work, though he never thought anything would come of the encounter. Todd was persistent in his pursuit of Steve. Soon they fell in love and moved in together. But during their years together as a couple, they had no gay friends in common.

Moreover, most of Steve's and Todd's friends were straight women. Now that Todd had asked for a divorce, Steve found companionship with women whom he loved dearly and who loved him in return. But he wasn't connected to any other gay men, even as acquaintances.

His coming to see me was a big step, since he didn't trust gay men very much—his only encounters had been in the bars and in the gyms where he'd worked out. Steve talked about his unwittingly homophobic belief that gay culture was just based on sex. He believed he'd never find another partner because he saw his meeting Todd as a fluke, a once-in-a-lifetime event that now was ending. He'd tried everything he could to convince Todd to stay, but to no avail. His partner wanted out, to date other men. He felt—wrongly!—that their inevitable power struggle (which I'll explain fully in Chapter 9) indicated that their relationship was over. Todd couldn't induce Steve to buy a house or to go out more in the gay community. So, after long consideration, he decided to end their relationship and not work through the power struggle.

Now Steve was alone, with no gay friends, feeling empty and isolated. I invited him to enter my gay men's therapy group. Due to constraints on his time and finances, he didn't want to make the weekly commitment. I also encouraged him to attend my gay men's workshop, which was less costly and time-consuming and also offered an opportunity for contacts with other gay men.

Steve declined. His work in therapy with me consisted of working through his grief over the loss of Todd and adjusting to a single life without any gay friends. He did start to date through personal ads in *Between the Lines,* our local gay newspaper. But these encounters only confirmed his belief that he had no hope of finding lasting love as a gay man.

As he began to feel less depressed, he came to his appointments less frequently. Finally, he admitted that money was the issue now that his partner had moved out and he was paying the rent by himself. He soon terminated therapy.

Steve's resistance to new friendships with gay men caused him a lot of problems. It contributed to an even longer period of grieving over the loss of his partner and only worsened his isolation. Many clients use lack of time and money as excuses to abandon their therapy. But I've noticed that people usually make time—and find the money—to do the things they really want to do. Steve resisted going to the emotional places he needed to. I suspect that from the start he'd never found a secure place for himself within his family. Because of his parents' neglect and emotional abuse, it seemed "normal" to Steve when his schoolmates treated him with the same disrespect.

On a conscious or unconscious level, peer perpetrators—of any age—often know whom they can pick on. Their victim might as well be wearing a neon sign on his forehead, but he doesn't know he's wearing it. If the child—or adult—never fights back, his predicament only gets worse.

Steve never fought back; he just took the abuse, which further damaged his self-esteem. Now, as an adult, he perpetuated the conditions of his isolation. He was extremely reluctant to socialize with others—particularly with gay men, who reminded him of the pain of Todd's rejection and the cruelty of his peers in his school days.

Breaking up is different for gay men. Straight men usually get sympathy from family and friends, who try to "fix up" the lonely guy. This generally doesn't happen for us, because our straight friends and family members usually don't know other gay men to fix us up with. Nor are they always eager to see us partnered! A single gay man is less conspicuous, so his family may be secretly relieved not to have to deal with his partner. But if he has other gay friends or a support group, they can invite him over for coffee, talk about past relationships and current problems, and provide the kind of mirroring and consolation that no straight friend could possibly offer.

By not allowing himself to maintain gay friends during his relationship, Steve had left himself vulnerable. Bars and gyms don't give an accurate picture of what all of gay life is like. They only parallel *straight* life at the bars and gyms, where shallow encounters and the expectation of speedy gratification are the norm.

Steve resisted gay men's group therapy, weekend workshops, and support groups because, unconsciously, he understood that participating in these activities would reawaken his feelings from childhood, when he didn't get acceptance from peers or family. The more I talked to him about this, the less often he came to therapy. He simply wasn't ready.

In the class I teach on gay and lesbian studies, I like to read excerpts from the chapter "Homosexual Love Relationships," from Joseph Nicolosi's misinformed *Reparative Therapy of Male Homosexuality: A New Clinical Approach*. It vividly depicts the abusive ways that our relationships are judged and viewed by heterosexist, homophobic, and misinformed people.

"Gay couplings are characteristically brief and very volatile, with much fighting, arguing, making-up again, and continual disappointments. They may take the form of intense romances, where the attraction remains primarily sexual, characterized by infatuation and never evolving into mature love; or else they settle into long-term friendships while maintaining outside affairs."[1]

Once, a heterosexual woman about 50 years old raised her hand and said, "While you were reading that, Joe, I couldn't think of whether you were talking about my first, second, or third marriage!"

The class roared. Everyone agreed that these problems are often found in heterosexual relationships as well.

The difference is our straight counterparts receive a lot more help, support, and education on how to make their relationships work. (Just visit your local bookstore to see how many guidebooks exist for heterosexual couples and how many there are for us.) Nicolosi does not address that, however. None of the reparative therapies ever examine why gay couples have problems. They stop with the explanation that it's simply because we're gay, not because of what's done to us for being gay.

Many gay men who come to my office play down their need to be in gay environments. They often talk about their desire to "blend in" and live a "mainstream" life where being gay isn't their primary identity. This is their personal choice, of course, but often these same men have difficulty finding gay friends and partners. Sadly, their internalized homophobia puts them in a bind: You can't expect to meet gay men if you never go to places where they're out and visible.

We have a parallel version of this syndrome within our own culture—straight women who choose to hang out primarily with gay men and their own girlfriends. They complain of not dating much, about not having boyfriends, and of their grief at being alone. I've always considered "fag hag" a brutal term—yet it's the label these women often give to themselves.

Like gay men who distance themselves from the gay community, they cultivate habits that are isolating and self-defeating. But there are deeper issues here—for both the straight women and the gay men they hang with. Up front are fears of intimacy and self-esteem. A woman who's attracted to men but also fears them may pal around with "safe" hunks who won't hit on her. It's a no-risk relationship, with all sexual tension drained out.

Meanwhile, because their gay friends are clearly out of reach, isolated gay men feel safe. And for any gay man with internalized homophobia, a straight woman is a crutch for his self-esteem: Spending time with her makes him feel better about himself and improves his image in society. He can avoid homophobia by hiding behind her and can receive heterosexual privileges from others who think he is straight.

No religious family would move to a neighborhood where the nearest church or synagogue was 100 miles away then complain about their isolation from others of their faith. This is the rationale for the "gay ghetto" where some men take comfort in the high proportion of other gay men. The goal isn't to limit your social spectrum but to end your isolation and increase the likelihood of meeting gay friends.

Another issue we have to face is our tendency to appropriate negative messages and judgments and to accept them as truths. In "Multiple Mirroring with Lesbian and Gay Couples," a chapter in *Healing in the Relational Paradigm*, Sharon Kleinberg and Patricia Zorn explain how internalized homophobia manifests itself in gay and lesbian couples.[2] They begin by debunking the widely held myth that gay couples cannot survive. During the power struggle, many gay couples assume this myth must be true. But all couples— gay and straight alike—go through this stage.

Zorn and Kleinberg address more subtle examples of internalized homophobia:

1. Trying to pass as straight even when it's safe to be out.
2. Not identifying yourself as gay even after you've been in a com mitted relationship for years.
3. Never announcing your anniversary to straight friends because anniversaries aren't as "important" for gay couples.
4. Avoiding public displays of affection even where it's safe to do so.
5. Criticizing a partner for looking too effeminate.

As we observed earlier, many gay men have spent their entire lives avoiding one another as much as they can for fear of being discovered and scorned. In a bar with loud music and alcohol, the emotional distance between gay men could not be greater.

Other, better ways to meet men include activities at gay community centers; gay-friendly religious services; running, bicycling, bowling, and swimming clubs; Gay Pride parades and Pridefest; gay vacation packages through travel agents; and personal ads on the Internet and in local newspapers. You can also volunteer for gay political and social groups such as Human Rights Campaign or find employment at a gay-friendly business.

If you can offer specialized services to these organizations, by all means do so. But don't forget, even a "menial" job like stuffing envelopes is an act of service that lets you begin to socialize with other gay men.

Dating can be a barbaric experience, for straight and gay folks alike. Participants don't know each other at the start and therefore lack any initial feelings of attachment. A number of my clients "hate" gay culture for being so visually oriented. I constantly remind them that this is a guy issue, not a gay issue. For better or worse, men generally look for partners who look good on the outside. Women do this too, of course. But from the earlier stages of dating, women tend to be attracted to more than just an attractive face or impressive body.

A client of mine proved this! He wrote a truthful personal ad, describing himself as "50 years old, overweight." He sent it to a mainstream newspaper, to run under the "Men Looking for Men" heading.

By mistake, the paper placed his ad under "Men Looking for Women." He received responses from 15 women interested in dating him. Then he called the paper and asked them to run it under the appropriate heading. When they did, he received not one response!

Women give men more leeway regarding physical appearance. Compared with their straight male counterparts, gay men are at a disadvantage: Prospective partners are less forgiving of a gay man's advancing age or protruding belly.

But don't give up! Many gay men take a valuable lesson from their lesbian counterparts, who often find themselves attracted to other women for reasons other than looks.

Many gay men come to my office anxious about their romantic

prospects because they are not young and buff. Because they don't look like circuit boys, they belittle themselves and fear that their odds of linking up with another gay man are low to zilch.

However, not all men are attracted to twinks, six-pack abs, or smooth-chested gym bunnies. A friend of mine moderates a Web site for gay personal ads. According to him, "I see quite a few posts saying, 'Looking for 50+,' and 'overweight OK.' Needless to say, I don't prune them after the usual two-week limit. They deserve to stay posted as long as the Web site survives!"

In his absurd comedy *The Ritz,* gay playwright Terrence McNally introduced a stereotype well known in the gay world: the chubby-chaser. A man I know was rejected on his first date for being *too* height-weight proportionate. The other guy shook his head: "Only guys built like cherubs turn me on." There's also the "bear" community, where being hairy and husky is a major turn-on.

Lesbian comedian Shan Carr, who primarily works in gay male settings, once joked that she used to feel bad about herself, compared to gay men. They were all so nicely built, worked out, and watched what they ate. Here she was overweight and snacking on fast food. Then she went to entertain at a bear convention and saw scads of men even heavier than she was. She screamed in delight, "I'm gonna get a bikini! For the first time, *I'm* the skinny bitch at the pool!"

There are even organizations dedicated to younger men attracted to older men. I once had a 40-year-old client who told me he doesn't look at a guy under 70! There's great diversity in our culture. You just have to get out there to find it. Yes, the search might be difficult, but that can make it even more rewarding.

I often find myself working as a dating coach as well as a psychotherapist. My clients deserve whatever I can give them! Look at your childhood, your adolescence, and your past relationships. Do you keep finding men, over and over, with the same traits of the people who raised you? Or with the same traits as men you've been with before? If you don't resolve the issue you'll keep suffering your way through miserable relationships.

According to Imago Relationship theory (more about that in the next chapter), we find different "actors" to read from our old childhood scripts. As adults, we keep seeking—and finding!—understudies to read stale dialogue from our past family relationships. This is why people often find themselves in work situations that remind them of childhood experiences, or with "friends" who treat them how relatives or schoolmates used to. Because this process is unconscious, it's imperative to make a *conscious* effort to stop recycling your past.

Clients who tell me, "I can't change it, so what's the point?" seldom realize they're rerunning yesterday's paradigms in the present.

Socially, we gay men can't always tell whether we're going out on a romantic date, or just as friends. I dated for 10 years—and this uncertainty drove me crazy! Sometimes I'd find a guy very attractive and ask him out—only to discover, many weeks and many "dates" later, that while I was falling in love he saw only a budding friendship!

It pays to remain close friends with men you've dated even after your romance has cooled. Yes, it can happen, with no resentment or jealousy. I once dated the rabbi who conducted the ceremony when Mike and I got married. Our best men were a couple, and I once dated one of them! Ironic, but it was such an honor to have these two be part of our ceremony. They both helped me find the right partner for me.

One of our best men was Jeff. I'd dated him about eight times, thought I never considered him my type. But, as with all of my other dating relationships, I approached him with an open mind.

At that time, I was adamant about not having sex until I felt comfortable. Jeff respected that. He was always courteous, and I began to really like him. He was stable, insightful, smart, and, like me, Jewish.

I started to have feelings for him. Then, one night, he said he was getting back together with another man he'd dated before—he wanted to try to make their relationship work. He liked me, he said, but his heart was pulling him toward this other man (who, I'm delighted to say, has been his partner for more than 10 years). But back then, I was devastated! I'd taken a risk and found myself attached to this guy who decided to drop me.

We had a ritual: After each date, we walked around the large pond near his condominium. Right then, I just wanted to get in my car, race home, and cry my heart out. But instead, I stretched myself and walked around the water with him. We talked about what had been nice about dating each other. He kissed me goodbye, and I drove home—calm and sad.

Over the next few years, I grew to appreciate what Jeff did. To my mind, he was a real mensch—strong, always honest with me, empathic, and respectful of what we'd had together during our eight dates. Now he's one of my best friends!

Yes, when someone says he's not interested in you, it hurts—but that's part of dating. Not every at-bat is a home run. It's more important, in my opinion, to treat others with the degree of respect Jeff showed me.

After our parting, I handled the rest of my dates the same way. The truth can hurt, but as one writer once joked, "It's Windex for the soul." It leaves things clearer and lets you forge a relationship as friends who honor each other.

When I went out with Mike for the first time, he asked me, "Is this a date?" That was so nice, innocent, and brave that it grabbed my heart. How many men would have the nerve to ask that question and risk being told no?

Of course my answer was yes.

The second time, before Mike and I went out to dinner early in the evening, he asked me, "Are were still dating?" Another honest, direct, and vulnerable question!

"My answer is yes—if you're still interested."

He was still interested. What if he hadn't been, or I hadn't? That's the unavoidable risk we all take. Most gay men have suffered in so many ways that they'll do anything to avoid rejection.

Even if you excel at what you do and get high praise from your bosses, coaches, and families, the prospect of rejection leaves your romantic heart at risk. But the alternatives—isolation and loneliness—are even scarier and more depressing.

I teach gay men to look at dating as a learning experience that teaches them how to turn negatives into positives. I know this isn't easy, but it's all about marketing oneself. The idea is to know the rules—and also to know when there really aren't any. Dating is about having fun while protecting your heart and ego. When you get rejected, it's not about your self-worth. As you recall from Chapter 1, judgments are 90% a reflection of the one doing the judging.

That may sound simplistic, but matters of the heart are never simple. I invite clients to venture into the dating arena with intentionality and consciousness. This strategy diminishes the chances of getting hurt—no matter the outcome—and allows you to learn more about yourself and the kind of men you want to meet.

Bypassing this leaves you stranded in emotional adolescence. During my own dating, I found that the men I chose—and who chose me—got better and better in terms of maturity, honesty, and integrity. Overall, I learned lots about myself. Who and what was right for me? Every OK guy I dated led me to a better guy. I learned from what I did—and didn't—enjoy about each person and experience. I became alert to those factors in my next relationship. I even formed friendships with some great men.

There are a few issues to approach cautiously. Clients often complain about the man who "wants a relationship." He might seduce you into thinking that he's relationship-oriented but—almost immediately—his behavior doesn't bear this out. You go out with friends. There he is at the bar, alone, looking to hook up. You hear rumors about his going to the baths. You confront him, and he denies that his behavior means anything. This doesn't mean he's "bad" or wrong, or even that he's lying to you. He may very well want a relationship, but he may not be ready for one. Also, he may not realize what it means to be in a relationship, or he may be unwilling to do the necessary work.

I encourage clients to talk to the other man about the lack of congruency between his words and his behavior - and about how they feel about it. Then I tell them to stop torturing themselves by listening only to his words. Move on! As an inspirational speaker once said, "Don't just observe the obvious—get the hell out of the way!

Another one to look out for is the man who just wants you for sex and nothing more. He may court you and flirt all night, saying you have nice eyes and a great personality. But afterward, you never see him again. Or if you do, he passes you by as if he's never seen you before. Obviously, this can be very hurtful—the more so if the experience was particularly pleasurable and you got your hopes up.

After encountering a number of men like this, I shifted from short-term, recreational dating to long-term, relationship-oriented dating. As I mentioned, I developed a cardinal rule—and boundary—for myself: No sex before I was ready. Yes, this was difficult to bring off. Many an attractive man passed me by, but that was OK with me. If he couldn't wait and didn't feel connected or interested enough, then I decided he wasn't right for me. No shame or blame on either of us! In this way I avoided the hurt of having sex with the guy only to have it turn out to be nothing.

When I share this with my clients, some look at me like I am crazy. "No sex! I could never do that!" I tell them, "You have to do what's right for you. That's what worked for me."

When you're looking for partners, another factor to consider is how far along you are in your own coming-out process. Many openly gay clients, sadly, find boyfriends who are just barely out of the closet. Still, they crave a relationship. I've found that if one man is in the early stages of coming out and his partner is further along, they're less likely to stay together.

Let's say that you're mostly out and living as a gay man in the fullest sense. You meet a guy who frets about what people might think about two men eating dinner together at a restaurant. Once he's your boyfriend, he never introduces you to his family. Even worse, he thinks it's weird for men to be romantic and playful outside the bedroom.

Beware! Differences in how *out* you both are can hinder the love you feel for each other.

Ted had been out of the closet his whole adult life. His relationship to Jonathan was his third and Jonathan's first. During their five years together, Ted wanted to live together, but Jonathan resisted. He ran a pet shop and wasn't yet out to his family or his business partner. He didn't plan to come out anytime soon and worried that living with Ted would be a red flag that he was gay, since they were both in their 30s.

This situation caused much friction when they got together on weekends. Whose apartment would they go to, given that one of them would have to pack a bag? Ted was frustrated and contemplated breaking off the relationship, even though he didn't want to. At Ted's insistence, he and Jonathan came to couples therapy with me.

Ultimately, Jonathan decided to talk to a younger cousin about his being gay and to bring Ted along to family functions. The cousin reacted negatively and told him never to bring up the subject again. Jonathan was devastated! Now he felt there was no way he could tell his immediate family—living with Ted was not an option. But Ted's parents welcomed Jonathan, and Ted resented not having the same opportunity with Jonathan's family.

They stayed in couples therapy for about three months, then canceled their last appointment and stopped coming. Not long afterward, Jonathan called me, weeping, to say that Ted had just ended their relationship. Jonathan reentered therapy with me, this time by himself. They had never lived together. Jonathan was still afraid to be seen with Ted, but now that their relationship was over he tearfully stated that he'd do anything to save it, including coming out more. But it was too late. This time, Ted was serious—he was through with Jonathan.

Now, at age 39, Jonathan felt scared and alone. He was finally facing himself. I stressed the importance of coming out. Jonathan finally saw how his closetedness was ruining his life. Ironically, he was now finally willing to do the work toward coming out that he was unable to do within his relationship with Ted—though he bitterly lamented the cost he'd had to pay.

If you don't feel good about being gay—or your boyfriend doesn't—then one of you will keep his distance, and you'll never feel close. As you'll see in Chapter 9, differences can help strengthen a relationship, but this particular one can be toxic. This is particularly true if the object of your affection, like Jonathan, isn't really interested in coming out at all.

Clients in the earlier stages of coming out complain of volatile, short-term relationships or of strong attractions to men who are either straight or married. What better way to keep emotional and physical distance?

Not that the partner who's farther along in the coming-out process can't help the other partner along. That can strengthen the relationship. A man in Stage One of coming out can fall in romantic love with another guy whom he admires for being even more out. But another problem I've seen: As the more closeted man grows, progressing through the later stages of coming out, he finds himself no longer attracted to his boyfriend. He sees him in a different, more realistic light. Maybe they have nothing more in common, there's no spark—and he no longer wants to date him! If their connection was based solely on "outness," consciously or not, their relationship is in jeopardy.

Don, a 45-year-old lawyer, had been dating his boyfriend for over a year. Up to that point, Don had been heterosexually married, with no children, and was about to make partner in his firm. He'd had very little time for himself and didn't come out until relatively late in his life. While venturing out to a gay bar, he'd met 26-year-old Mario, who was *very* much out of the closet. Don didn't like it that Mario frequented the bars and drank a lot, but he was drawn to Mario's relaxed, natural manner—and to how obviously comfortable Mario was about being gay.

Yes, their age differences could be an issue. But Don rationalized that in "gay years," he too was around 25 emotionally. With this frame of mind, he assumed they were a good match.

Don spent most of his time with Mario and his bar friends, who were wild and drank heavily. One time, Mario verbally abused Don in front of his friends and wouldn't stop, even at Don's insistence. Mario would drive recklessly, with Don in the passenger seat fearing for his life. Because he'd lent Mario money, Don described himself to me as a "sugar daddy" and a "cash cow."

I encouraged Don to enter my gay men's group therapy, to experience men who were gay and also dealing with other issues. Don accepted and for two years, on a weekly basis, he began to examine his past.

A Sunday painter, Don was drawn to abstract art. But Don's mother hid his interest in arts from her husband, who was annoyed at his son's "artsy, effeminate" bent. When Don was older, attending classes at a fine arts academy on weekends, his father was so embarrassed that he'd drop Don off four blocks away because he was afraid to be seen delivering his son to a "sissy" academy.

It was now obvious to Don why he had disowned the same aspects of himself that his father had disowned. At 45, he decided, No more! But while coming out, he'd met Mario, who treated him much the same way his family had. (As we've learned, we all tend to replay familiar scripts simply *because* they're familiar—even if they flopped the first time around.)

Mario was unwilling to change his behavior. Still Don was drawn to him. Yet as Don came out more and more, he found his relationship with Mario diminishing in importance. Ultimately, Don passed through all six stages and found the courage to break with Mario. He then met a man closer to his own age, both chronologically and emotionally, who had shared many of the same experiences. They developed a relationship, and Don left therapy. We agreed he was going in the right direction. May-December relationships can thrive only if both partners are willing to grow and to help each other pass through emotional stages.

Another trap lies in waiting for the nurturing type or looking for someone who wants to be nurtured. As they said on *Seinfeld,* not that there's anything wrong with that! But when Don said that he was Mario's sugar daddy, he should have heard some warning bells in his own head. Many men and women, gay and straight, don't want to be accountable or responsible. They seek a partner or "long-term caretaker" to do it all for them.

The following questions may seem petty, but your answers can be symptomatic of problems to come:

1. Who pays for your meal?
2. Do you split the check?
3. Does he offer—ever?
4. Who phones whom? Is it back and forth, or are you always leaving messages on his answering machine?
5. Who makes plans? Is it mutual?
6. Does he ask you questions and listen to your answers, or use them as a springboard to talk about himself?
7. Does he listen? If not, he's probably not ready to relate, reciprocate, and share.

Chapter 5 covered the dangers and dynamics of sexual addiction. Here, it's your job to ensure that you're free from addictive patterns and chemicals and that your dating partner is too. As one of my clients said of his own drinking while he was initially dating, "It was like having a joker in the deck." Too often, men find a boyfriend who drinks or does drugs, and they say to themselves, "This too will pass—it's only a phase."

It's not that simple. If the guy you are dating has any type of untreated addiction, it will only get worse as you become closer. Talk to him about your observations and don't let it drop. It's up to you to see whether he answers with rationalizations, says he'll stop but doesn't, or tries to limit his drinks unsuccessfully. You need to know whether the use interferes in his life or your relationship. Again, focus on behaviors, not on what is said.

Many clients say they knew a boyfriend was stringing them along, or seeing other men, while telling them otherwise. Yet they kept on seeing this same man for fear of having no one at all. Gay or straight, anyone who strings someone else along is self-centered, concerned only about himself, with little or no regard for others. (Ironically, hustlers and male escorts—men who frankly sell their favors for money—are typically thoughtful and considerate of their clients' feelings!) The "pretty" guy preys on "victims" with low self-esteem, because he's confident that he won't be rejected. The very worst of this type is the sociopath who just likes to make trouble and watch people squirm. Many gay men who fear they're too old and/or unattractive link up with narcissistic men like this because they believe they deserve no better.

When clients are dating, I always coach them to be direct and honest. It's hard enough to handle all the issues they must face during the dating process. Integrity isn't just a moral issue—it saves valuable time! If you're not really attracted to a man, let him know (in a kind way) that you're not interested. Yes, he might feel hurt, particularly if he likes you. But that's OK. Let *him* move on. Making him feel more "comfortable" by giving him a line ("I'll call you sometime" or "This could be a great friendship") and then never calling back could be more hurtful still. Not everyone gets a hint—so be direct!

If you want to attract a man of integrity, then it is important to behave like one yourself. You should focus not only on others' behaviors matching their words, but on your own as well. Be who you say you are. Follow your words with actions.

Anonymous sexual encounters offer you adventures in which you can try out new things, but so can dating—in emotional, risk-taking ways. On either playing field you can get rejected. And just as cruising helps to refine your hookup skills, each date lets you clarify your emotional goals.

While dating, I did all kinds of things I'd never have done otherwise. I went boating and camping with a guy who loved the outdoors. I'd never done those things before, and I found they were fun. Other men I dated showed me fine dining experiences, different ways to dress, and more rewarding ways to look at life. I learned about good wines. I learned that dating a man who was too much like me could be boring, even horrifying. I needed a calmer homebody type, not an anxious, overextended social guy. Overall, I acquired the skills and confidence to maintain a rewarding relationship. Again, discover what works and what doesn't work—for *you*. Here are some tips:

1. Set aside your pride. Dating is not for the hypersensitive. Even if the guy isn't interested in you because of how you look or how you are in bed, remember that's about him and his desires, not about

you. Another guy may want you because of the very thing this guy doesn't care for. Recognize that nothing is personal. Assure yourself that there's nothing wrong with you.

2. Step out of your own way. Listen to the guy's judgments of you, remembering they're 90% about him! However, there may be some kernel of truth to what he's saying. Hear his words, whatever they may be, and decide for yourself what you think about them.

3. Never play games. If you're not sure where the relationship is heading, or what his intentions are, be direct: "I really like you and would like to see more of you" or "When two men go out, it's hard to know if it's a date. I'd like it to be. Would you?"

4. Be vulnerable. With your feelings put aside and protected, you can allow yourself to take risks. Do and say things you normally wouldn't. Use this as an opportunity to find out how you want to be in a relationship.

5. Don't let another guy play games or be indirect. Getting mixed signals? "You say this, but you do that. It confuses me. Can you tell me how you feel about me?" If after some dialogue he won't be direct, then he's not the guy for you.

6. Never judge either of you as right or wrong, good or bad. When dating isn't going well, it's easy and common for people to want to make things black and white. This is a dead-end road. Everyone has his own way of communicating and his own level of awareness, as you'll discover when you date different men. If that dating situation isn't working out for you, just move on to the next guy; don't label someone bad just because he's different.

7. Stay visible. Many of my clients struggle to find men to date because they're not involved in the gay community. Go to the gay and lesbian community center, get on committees and boards, volunteer your time for gay organizations, help with a mailing, go to fund-raisers. This is where active, confident gay men are.

8. Even if (especially if!) things go badly, see dating as a fun experience, an adventure. This lesson was very hard for me. I dated lots of interesting characters for 10 years before I met my partner. Finally, during the last three years of dating, I let myself

have fun—and learned a lot. Each guy I dated taught me something different and exposed me to new things in my life, for which I'm grateful.

9. Learn from each dating relationship. Observe yourself and reflect on what went well and what didn't. Were you open, honest, and direct? Did you hold back your thoughts and feelings just to make the relationship work? Were you moving too fast? Too slow?

10. Force yourself to approach men. Don't wait to be approached. If I approached a guy, especially in front of his friends, and struck up a conversation, it was worth the risk. How else would I ever know whether the encounter might turn into anything?

If the conversation didn't go well, I'd keep asking questions to break the ice. People like to talk about themselves. Being a therapist, I'm genuinely interested in learning about people.

But beware! Some men like to talk exclusively about themselves. If the conversation doesn't eventually move back to you, consider this a red flag. For many guys, everything you say about yourself becomes a prompt for something about themselves.

11. Put ads on gay Web sites and in local gay newspapers. I've counseled lots of men who found rewarding dating partners and long-term relationships that way.

12. Learn to laugh about some of the experiences you are having. Laugh at yourself for the blunders you made. Once I dated a guy who drew stares wherever we went. At first I thought I was imagining it and asked whether he noticed it too. He initially denied it, then later confirmed it, but he wouldn't say why. Was he on a wanted list? In the news for some scandal? Only later did I learn he was mayor of the city we were in! Because he'd lied about his job, I cut short our dating. Later, I couldn't stop laughing at the lengths he went to not to tell me.

One time I hosted a dinner party. During a quiet moment, a man I was dating told everyone he was a top. I was horrified! We hadn't yet had sex or even talked about it, but after that my guests must have assumed I was a bottom. While there is nothing wrong with that, I would rather they not know anything, verified or not, about me sexually! The lesson: Laugh, then move on.

References

1. Joseph Nicolosi, *Reparative Therapy of Male Homosexuality: A New Clinical Approach.* Northvale, NJ: Jason Aronson (1997).

2. Sharon Kleinberg and Patricia Zorn, "Multiple Mirroring With Lesbian and Gay Couples: From Peoria to P-Town," in *Healing in the Relational Paradigm: The Imago Relationship Therapy Casebook,* edited by Wade Luquet and Mo Therese Hannah. Washington, D.C.: Brunner-Routledge (1998).

Chapter 9
Understand the Stages of Love

MY PARTNER AND MY FATHER HAVE THE SAME NAME—
DADDY!
—comedian Eddie Sarfaty

Jokes like this make us laugh because they reveal poignant truths about our experience as gay men. And unless you take those truths seriously, they can interfere with your ability to find and keep a relationship.

Straight or gay, we all long for contact and connection with one another. We yearn to be in lasting, adult love relationships. My clients and my friends talk constantly about their longings and yearnings to find a partner. "With no significant other," they say, "my life isn't complete." Of course, you'll hear the same remarks from our heterosexual counterparts. But gay men who want to find a partner have a few extra hurdles and barriers.

Role Models

When my clients go to gay bars and social events and see an overwhelming majority of single—or at least seemingly unattached—men, they conclude that gay couplehood is rare, if not impossible. At clubs, at marches—even at my weekend workshops and therapy groups!—single gay men are far more visible than partnered gay couples. This leads to the logical but totally inaccurate assumption that gay couples simply don't exist.

Compared with the heterosexual community, where romantic and married couples regularly go out together, gay relationships—short- or long-term—are not nearly so visible. Unfortunately, many of the "obvious" gay couples who go to bars or clubs together are in sexually open relationships. They simply enjoy the ego-boost when other men find their partners attractive. They may flirt so heavily it's hard to tell whether they're really a couple.

Ironically, gay men are regularly accused of being promiscuous, yet when we want our monogamous relationships to be valued and legalized, we're told that we're wrong for even asking! Dr. Laura, the radio talk show host, called it a "sadness" that anyone would want to partner with the same gender.

One night, back when I was single, I'd just ended a short relationship. I returned home from a gay bar, still reeking of tobacco smoke, partially deafened by the loud music, and feeling fairly depressed. A well-meaning family member was there to greet me. After I told her of my hopelessness about finding Mr. Right, she offered me some advice: "Maybe you'll meet lots of men and have multiple relationships throughout your life. Just enjoy the good times with them. When they end, expect it and move on."

At the time, her remark made me feel nurtured and comforted. Over time, however, I came to understand her words as products of ignorance and homonegativity. I couldn't imagine her "reassuring" my sister by telling her, "Maybe you'll have many boyfriends and husbands throughout your life. Just enjoy each one. When it ends, move on."

What I needed to hear was exactly what a heterosexual person needs to hear: "Hey! Don't worry. Mr. Right *is* out there. In fact, there are quite a few Mr. Rights, and you can settle down with one—if that's really what you want. The bars aren't the best place to meet someone. Keep trying, and go to more social events that aren't bar-related. You deserve fidelity and true love."

That's what I needed to hear that night, and that's what I want gay men to get from this chapter.

Support from Family and Friends

Our society tends to see relationships, gay and straight alike, as disposable. More than half of heterosexual marriages end in divorce; when a relationship runs into trouble, many participants decide to abort it and try for a better one. In fact, friends and relatives who weren't 100% behind the union from the start often encourage couples to break things off rather than to stay in the partnership. There are countless instances where disapproving parents wait for the first whiff of trouble then use it as an excuse to challenge their heterosexual son's or daughter's commitment to a partner whom they never really liked in the first place. For gay relationships, that goes double.

Those who hear about marital counseling and couples therapy say, "Relationships shouldn't be so much work." But relationships, especially the good ones, are a *lot* of work. The idea that any problem indicates a bad relationship isn't true—except when domestic violence is involved, or when one partner's addicted to drugs, alcohol, sex, or gambling and won't seek treatment. Violence and addiction indicate that you need to seek a therapist for immediate help.

Understanding What Relationships Really Are

A most important question: Are you looking for Mr. Right or Mr. Right Now? So many of my clients talk about wanting a partner, but their efforts and behaviors don't reflect that. They actually do all they can to avoid seeing someone long-term. They want a relationship, but on an unconscious level they see the work involved as scary, if not terrifying.

We can blame failed relationships on society, families, and friends all we want, but the bottom line is that we have to look within ourselves. Relationships force us to look at the darkest parts of who we are—as well as the most loving parts that exist in us.

Far too many gay men enter adult love relationships with the unspoken, internalized conviction that they're inherently damaged and flawed. Their self-doubt becomes a self-fulfilling prophecy, and they project their own perceived weaknesses onto their partners.

Meanwhile, there's also that imprinted expectation, conscious or not, that the relationship won't last. Any wonder that problems arise?

Few of us realize that problems are *supposed* to happen in a relationship and that they can speed us to great personal healing. For the physical body, moderate stress—as in brisk walking—helps leg bones stay solid and healthy. Just so for a relationship: Minor problems can help the bond strengthen and grow.

As a therapist, the most important training I ever received was Imago Relationship Therapy (or IRT), as developed by Harville Hendrix. In *Getting the Love You Want: A Guide for Couples,* Hendrix outlines the stages of love and describes what attracts us to potential partners in the first place. Although his book's geared toward heterosexuals, his theory applies to everyone.

Most relationship books, such as John Gray's *Men Are From Mars, Women Are From Venus* and Deborah Tannen's *You Just Don't Understand,* focus on differences between men and women. Hendrix emphasizes the individual, not gender, which makes his model perfect for gay and lesbian relationships as well.[1]

Imago is the Latin word *image.* Each of us assembles and creates an *imago* from both the positive and negative traits of our mother, father, and any other primary caretaker we had when we were growing up. The *imago* is the blueprint of the person we want to be in a committed, intimate relationship. Consciously or otherwise, we project this composite picture or image onto prospective partners, to see if they fit.

Parts of our *imago* can also be assembled from the community we grew up in, the religion we were taught, and from any important teacher, coach, or institution that left a profound impact on us while we were growing up. This composite image becomes a kind of treasure map that directs our search for adult love. We seek what feels familiar and therefore "safe"—even if it might seem exotic to someone else. Therefore we look for someone who reminds us of both the best and the worst traits of our parents and primary caretakers. And this is as it should be because, unromantic as it may sound, we partner to heal ourselves and to complete the unfinished business of childhood. Because our original wounding—and for gay men, that includes heterosexism and homophobia—occurred in the relationships with the people who raised us, our healing must also occur in the context of a relationship.

Some people have difficulty with that concept because "wounding" feels too strong. I always ask them whether "negative influencing" fits better. Others feel that they did not have any childhood wounding at all. I tell them to pick up any Developmental Psychology 101 book and see all the developmental tasks one has to go through to survive childhood. No one escapes without some negative influencing. Simply having a sibling born can be traumatic because you're no longer the number 1 child. No parents can raise a child perfectly; how they impact us shows up in our later relationships.

Of course, you're not aware of these unconscious processes at work. You see a guy you're attracted to and say to yourself, "Wow, he is hot! I like his smile, his butt, his whatever!" Meanwhile, your unconscious mind is saying, "Wow, familiar love! That's someone who reminds me of my Mommy and Daddy. I'm going over there!"

If you ever want to prove this phenomenon, just talk to any adult child of an alcoholic. He'll tell you that there can be 499 sober people in a room and he'll zero in on the one alcoholic. That person hardly has to say a word for the child of an alcoholic to feel an attraction. (Similarly, a famed screen actress married—and later divorced—a homosexual film director. Some twenty years later, their daughter, herself an actress, married—and later divorced—a gay songwriter and performer who eventually died of AIDS.)

Imagine that your childhood was like a Broadway smash hit that ran year after year. However, when the play went on the road, the original cast had to be replaced. The script remained the same, but the actors who played the leads and acted out the story were entirely different people. When we grow into adulthood and take our "show" on the road, we choose partners, friends, and even coworkers who can take over the roles of our mothers, fathers, ex-partners, and siblings to help us recycle our childhood, for better and for worse.

For years, I've heard women—both in therapy and in conversation—complain that every man wants to be married to his mother. Well, in theory, being gay solved that problem for me! I knew I didn't want to be married to my mother or anyone like her, so I thought I was exempt. In my relationships with men, I suspected that more than likely I'd have to deal with my father (with whom I didn't have a great relationship). Not so! In our *imago* searching, gender is not the issue. I picked a man who carries the positive and negative traits of both my mother and father.

Of course, it's the negative traits of your more dominant parent—the one who affected you most—that begin to interfere with the relationship. You'll find yourself seeking to resolve issues from your childhood—now, in your current relationship. The goal is to find a facsimile of your mother and father in a man who will provoke you like your mother and father did, but who's willing to modify his behavior to stop rewounding you.

Again, our participation in this grand drama is unconscious. However, the more you know about the process, the more mindful you become, and the better choices you make in selecting a partner. If you are already in a relationship this wisdom comes as a great relief. When conflict arises, you may assume it means you're with the wrong person. Not so!

The *right* partner is willing to change with you, knowing that this willingness to change will help him as well. Imago theory teaches that our partners hold the blueprint for our own personal growth. What we need most from our partners is often the hardest thing for them to give us. It is hard because the very thing we are asking them to give is often what they need to do for themselves.

For example, an Imago therapist once talked about how her lecturing and teaching around the country took her away from her husband and made her feel isolated and detached. She asked whether he'd be willing to call her every day during the one month she was gone. He resisted, saying, "My schedule is too busy."

She told her husband she felt ignored and neglected and that it would be healing for him do this for her, just for that one month.

Ultimately he agreed; he called her every day to tell her he missed her and loved her. She began to feel more emotionally secure about him and, toward the middle of the month, thanked him for gifting her with his calls. Eventually she no longer needed them.

"But I don't want to stop," he replied. "I like calling you every day. It makes me feel more connected to you as well."

They both laughed. He also received a missing piece of childhood intimacy that he'd never have recovered otherwise. This is why it's important to be as attentive to your partner's needs as he is to yours. You both can benefit when each of you gives the other what he needs most.

Mike and I met in 1993. I'd recently had some short-term dating relationships that had lasted no longer than three or four months, and I didn't know what I was doing wrong. I'd been in therapy myself, had been trained as a therapist, and still couldn't identify why I couldn't find Mr. Right. With earlier Imago training, maybe I could have spared myself some years of turbulence. I'd meet men who were narcissistic and inconsiderate—self-absorbed bully types. Yet they didn't need to say a word for me to feel their energy and be drawn to them. I would tell myself, "It was his looks."

Now I know there was more to it. Every time I started dating one of these men to whom I was wildly attracted, he'd tell me how angry I was! I'd respond by saying that *he* was the one making me so angry, and if he'd just change his behavior I'd calm down. Ultimately—obviously!—this scenario wouldn't work, and one of us would end the relationship.

From what I've learned in IRT, I now understand why I was drawn to bullies. First, while I was growing up, boys in school taunted and humiliated me. I never stood up for myself because I didn't know how. I just took it. No one taught me how to protect myself. My parents divorced when I was 3, and because of my father's absence and neglect, I was left with just my mother, who was the more dominant of the two. At home, her motto was "My way or the highway." Again, I chose to acquiesce. My sister didn't—and our mother punished her regularly for not complying. So these narcissistic types I dated were quite right: Yes, I was angry. But they didn't deserve my anger, because it wasn't meant for them. It was unresolved rage toward my mother and father and those childhood bullies.

In relationships, we regress to a time when we as children were taught to be quiet and to accept whatever our larger, stronger counterparts dished out. We don't know this on any conscious level, so we assume any problems we experience arise from the current relationship. In most cases, the relationship simply triggers memories and unresolved issues from a bygone time.

If our parents wounded us (or otherwise negatively influenced us), then they are the ones who can best help us to heal most deeply. However, a primary love partner who matches their traits can serve as their stand-in. Healing takes place when the partner we select says, in effect, "I can see I've hurt you, and unlike your parents I'm willing to modify my behavior." In my case, if any of those self-absorbed men I dated had been willing to say, "Joe, sorry I disappointed you. I can see your point and am willing to consider your needs more," then I could have started to heal the pain from my childhood. Mike, my partner, was the first man I dated who finally did this, and he grabbed my heart.

Mark and Barry, both in their early 30s, had been together as a couple for six years. They came to therapy because neither felt safe sharing his feelings with the other. This is a common problem for couples: When communication breaks down, they lose the essential experience of safety and trust.

Mark came from a family of lower socioeconomic status. When he was young, his father abandoned the family, leaving Mark's mother to raise him and his two siblings. She dated violent men who would beat her. When Mark was 11 years old, one of her boyfriends stabbed another man in his presence. Money was tight, and his mother worried constantly about how to pay the bills. Many nights she would stay out, leaving Mark, the oldest, to care for the other two children. Since his father was gone, being the "man of the house" made him feel privileged and important. His mother often called him her "little man." He was determined to comply with her wishes and not to give her any more concerns—and in doing so, he denied the violence around him.

From a very young age Mark knew he was gay and figured that becoming the "best little boy" would be a great cover. His mother would never notice—or even question—his sexuality. Consequently, Mark never said no to his mother and never learned to build appropriate boundaries.

Barry's mother died when he was very young. His older brother was detached, kept to himself, and resisted any contact with Barry. His father, a compulsive gambler, would sneak out of the house in the middle of the night to play poker. Later, Barry's father married a woman who was maternal and loving toward Barry, whom he began to consider a mother figure. But she and Barry's father didn't get along. One day she told Barry she was divorcing his father and left. Once again, he felt abandoned and fearful.

Early on, he'd learned to take care of himself and not to trust people. After he formed strong attachments, the most important people in his life had abandoned him. Later, as you can guess, he often entered relationships with men who would suddenly leave him— giving Barry no clue as to why.

In therapy, Mark claimed that Barry was making too many demands of him. If he didn't do things the way Barry wanted, he felt that Barry became unreasonable. For his part, Barry felt frustrated because when Mark was upset, he wouldn't admit it. Barry would find out only later, when a quick, effective solution was no longer possible.

Mark stated that Barry should "just know" his needs, without having to be told. But Barry couldn't know, of course—and, weeks after the event had passed, he would feel blindsided by Mark's anger. Then, unfortunately, Barry would sweep his own feelings under the carpet, fearing that if he showed his hurt and confusion, Mark might abandon him. This was their core argument. They fought over different situations, but it always came down to the same issue: Mark felt Barry was too demanding, and Barry didn't realize when he'd upset Mark.

I offered them the Imago explanation of how past conflicts often get recycled in adult relationships—usually in disguised form. I showed Mark how he projected a childhood wish onto Barry by assuming that Barry should intuit his needs without being told.

This is a common issue in relationships, gay and straight alike. I often hear one partner tell the other, "I shouldn't have to tell you. You should just know."

I always warn that this is dangerous. The only time you shouldn't have to tell someone your specific needs is in childhood—infancy in particular. As adults, we must explain our needs, preferences, and priorities. Otherwise, how—short of detective work or ESP—can our partners ever understand us?

Mark had to verbalize his own needs first, then get Barry to meet them. He also needed to set boundaries for himself and say when he felt that Barry was making too many demands. Neither of these was a skill he'd learned in childhood. Mark's mother was emotionally and often physically unavailable, which had kept him busy meeting everyone's needs but his own. Consequently he tried to get his partner to give him what his mother never did. The problem was that his partner could not know his needs unless Mark articulated them.

Burdening your partner to meet *all* of your unmet childhood needs is of course inappropriate; nevertheless, it is normal for most of us to try. Understanding this typical process helped Mark to identify his own needs and to communicate them to Barry—who became compassionate when he realized Mark's silences stemmed from his childhood. Barry saw he was simply triggering a sensitivity (a psychological "allergy," if you will) that Mark had developed long ago. The problem wasn't Barry's fault, as he had originally thought (and as Mark had told him).

For his part, Barry learned that he was recycling the pain of losing two women he'd been very attached to—his mother and stepmother—and the neglect of his distant, gambler father. Barry kept his fears of conflict and abandonment to himself, dealt with them internally, and didn't communicate them to Mark. To make their relationship work, Barry's challenge was to risk voicing his needs and to face his fears that Mark might leave him.

Now that Mark understood where Barry's trauma had originated, he was more understanding and reassured Barry that a passing conflict wouldn't make him want to break up. As you can imagine, these insights were wonderfully liberating for them both. Barry and Mark started creating safety for each other. Their communication improved, and their connection to each other deepened.

Unconsciously, we also search for people who display parts of ourselves that we have denied or disowned. Thus, your "ideal" partner may mirror aspects of yourself that are missing, distorted by defenses, and—at least for now—consciously lost.

When I met Mike, I immediately loved how peaceful and calm he was—so different from what I'd grown up with. I come from a very bold, forthright family. Everyone says whatever is on his or her mind, with no regard for others' feelings. Around them, I never knew when an argument was going to break out. Had I been quiet and easygoing, I'd have been bulldozed—so my tranquil, placid side went into hiding.

But Mike's family wasn't emotional and demonstrative. In me, he recognized the part of himself that yearned to argue or show strong emotion. He'd tell me, "You are so passionate, vibrant, and alive." So our lost parts met each other, along with familiar love from our childhood caretakers. We mirrored each other's *imago* without even knowing it.

This is also "shadow work," of course, in the language of Carl Jung and Robert Bly. My peaceful self was in shadow, as was Mike's emotional self. Our two shadows met and came out of hiding into the light. In essence, it is like uncovering buried treasure.

The goal of Imago Therapy is to establish committed, conscious, intimate relationships by aligning the conscious mind (which usually seeks happiness and good feelings) with the agenda of the unconscious mind, which seeks healing and growth. I love that IRT puts a positive spin on relationship problems that would otherwise seem impossible.

Almost all of us enter relationships through the wide, splendid gateway of *romantic love*. Movies, books, television, and pop music all celebrate the infatuation period when all the lights are on. Every positive detail is vivid and visible. It all feels so great!

For lesbians and gays, it's a time of even greater importance. This is when we realize we have found something (more precisely, someone) that we were told we couldn't ever have. We feel so lucky, fulfilled, and finally authentic. We've waited a lifetime for a connection like this! We don't want it to end. During this stage, which our society calls "true love," everyone—gays, lesbians, and straights alike—reports feelings of elation, exhilaration, and euphoria.

Three archetypal feelings offer a glimpse into the unconscious realm of romantic love:

1. *"I know we just met, but I feel I have always known you."*

People feel this way because their unconscious minds recognize the other's positive and negative traits. In a sense, then, they really have "always known" the person. There is a selection process going on.

Because your unconscious doesn't know the difference between past and present, you really do feel you've "always" known someone who resembles a familiar primary caretaker.

2. *"When I'm with you, I feel whole and complete."*

We feel whole when we meet someone who expresses the "lost" parts of ourselves that have been disowned or denied.

3. *"I can't live without you."*

This is an unconscious transfer of responsibility for our very survival from our parents to a partner. Unconsciously, we fear that if the partner leaves, we'll lose our lives. It's a primitive feeling. Children know that if their parents abandon them, they can't survive. But in adulthood, the unconscious mind doesn't recognize the difference when a partner leaves.

These feelings are strongest when both partners are physically together. During this time, they can operate on less sleep. Indeed, during this time, infatuated people will say they feel drugged. If they've been depressed before, they now report being less so. If they suffer from addictions, they'll experience diminished craving or even feel "cured." Their sex drive will increase to match their partner's.

There's more going on here: The experience of falling in love produces a natural amphetamine called phenalethalamine (PEA). In Chapter 5 we talked about PEA being released during sexual arousal. It also occurs during romantic love. When you're in love, you actually *are* drugged, without realizing it! When PEA is first released, it's at its most potent, which is why people never forget their first love. But recall this is also what promotes sex and love addiction. Problem is, each time it is released it's less powerful and lasts for a shorter period of time. It's not meant to last! Its only purpose is to connect two otherwise incompatible people, bond them, and make them willing to stay together so that each can help heal the other.

Many gay men seek nothing beyond the PEA experience. After it wears off, they complain that a relationship shouldn't be "so much work," and they're off to a new man. With heterosexual couples, by the time the PEA wears off, they are often engaged, with marriage and children following soon after. Not that these are the best of reasons to stay in a relationship, but they are factors that help heterosexual couples stay committed. Gay men usually don't have these same anchors to keep them steadfast.

Even so, infatuation isn't real love, much less "true love." It's only nature's way of bringing two humans together. It's supposed to happen—but also, for gays and straights alike, it's supposed to come to an end. (Most straight people don't know this, as you can see from the divorce rate.) And when it does end, sometimes it plunges gay men into even greater despair.

Too often, we enter a relationship believing that heterosexual relationships are generally superior to ours and that gay relationships don't last. So when a gay romance does end, it seems like a confirmation of the myth that love and romance are reserved for heterosexuals only and that gays cannot enjoy lasting love.

No one tells us that this phenomenon is universal! Romantic love is supposed to end—for everyone. PEA only makes staying together easier at first—before the necessary work begins.

Even so, when lightning strikes, many gay men do everything they can do to hang on to the man who inspired it. Gay partners sometimes break up and get back together many times because their reunion triggers a fresh dose of PEA. After a period of absence, both recall the thrill of their first meeting and say, "Let's do it again!" This explains the phenomenon of couples who divorce and then remarry almost habitually.

One way men, gay and straight, try to maintain this romantic high is by having (though not necessarily enjoying!) sex outside of the relationship. The sheer thrill of the hunt reawakens that PEA high, which they can then bring back home. Still another way to reawaken the PEA high is to invite other sex partners into the relationship. This is not a mature strategy and only postpones the inevitable power struggle.

That's the next stage of a relationship after romantic love ends. The *power struggle* also has a finite duration—thankfully, because this phase doesn't feel so good. Disillusionment arises. It's here that you become most acutely aware of the differences between yourself and your new partner.

As soon as we decide to make more of an investment in the person we're in romantic love with, the PEA wears off. If one partner was depressed before, he returns to his depressed state. If he enjoyed a higher sex drive during PEA, he reverts to a lower libido. He returns to "business as usual." Most people, unaware of this unconscious process, blame themselves—or more often, their partners—for their diminished interest. They deserve to be educated about the biological process of romantic love.

When the power struggle begins, partners say, in ascending order of commitment:

1. "Let's buy something together."
2. "Let's only see each other and stop dating other people."
3. "Let's take a vacation together."

4. "Let's move in together—or talk about the possibility."
5. "Let's get married [or engaged]."

When Mike and I started talking about living together (before I knew about Imago) we immediately started fighting. Where were we going to live? What furniture would be in the house? I'm not superficial or materialistic, but all of a sudden these details mattered to me—enormously. He wasn't going to let go of his vision, and neither was I. Even though we argued about furniture and housing, those weren't the real problem.

That's normal too: Couples usually argue over things that are not the core issue. The unconscious finds a way to disguise the real problems with more innocuous, seemingly unimportant matters.

The power struggle, then, is the second stage of relationships. Many couples never reach the end of the power struggle because they don't know how to navigate their way through.

The context of the power struggle is coded material. Deciphering it, you'll find information to help you to know yourselves better—as individuals and as a couple.

Most of the emotions we attach to any problem are connected to the past. Once you and your partner see that, there's more willingness on both sides to address the situation differently. That isn't always the outcome, but there's a much better chance of getting there than through other ways of handling conflict.

Mike and I kept arguing about chairs and sofas until we got to the root of the problem—on both sides. I was raised in a family where, in order to survive, I had to set aside my sense of self. So when Mike suggested that I move into *his* house with *his* possessions, I was transported back to a time when I was told that my needs didn't matter. That wasn't at all what Mike was saying to me, but I was unknowingly projecting that onto him. I became defensive and fought back. I hadn't been able to do that in childhood, but now I could argue for my needs, and that's exactly what I did. The problem was, I consciously thought the issue was about the house and furniture and not my sense of self.

Once I knew this, I pushed for my needs in other ways and encouraged Mike to meet them in a compassionate and understanding way. He realized our conflict was not about him at all but came from another time in my life, which helped him to see my point of view.

Fortunately I discovered the real issue in time for us to work it out. Many others are not so lucky and break up without ever learning what they were really arguing about.

In romantic love, our similarities connect us. PEA helps us bond—for a while. But during the power struggle we're disconnected by the very differences we thought we could overlook. Nature gave us help in the romantic stage, but dropped us off without a textbook during the power struggle. That's why a higher power made Imago therapists!

The power struggle begins in earnest with the realization that your partner can't or won't meet all your needs, as you originally expected. (Back in the romantic love phase, he may even have promised to do so.) And so old hurts and resentments reawaken. Mostly, these are old hurts from childhood, but they can also arise from unresolved conflicts in past relationships.

Some have theorized that we tend to re-create our first adolescent crush. That first release of PEA can be so strong as to imprint another template onto your Imago ideal. That person then becomes "our type," and we tend to be attracted to men who look and behave like him. If that crucial first infatuation ended badly, there's a good chance that we'll unconsciously try to resolve the kinks in that first relationship with any later stand-in.

During the power struggle stage, you'll hear statements like: "You know what I need! I don't have to tell you, and I shouldn't have to!" Or, "You have what I need, but you won't give it to me."

After the romantic period ends, of course, sex drives fall back to normal. The person with the higher libido may say, "You were more sexual when we first met. It was just a ploy to get me to move in with you." In other words, *You have what I need, but you won't give it to me.* This "what" usually reflects some childhood need that went unmet—not sex, of course, but usually attention and responsiveness from a caregiver.

During the romantic stage, we began to feel a sense of entitlement to whatever we want from our partner, as if he owes us. (Again, this is a regression to the blissful days of infancy, when an ideal caregiver was quick to answer our every complaint.) Now we find our partner different than we thought he was—and for that, of course, we blame him. The very things that attracted us to our partners become things we dislike. Qualities we once adored, now we cannot bear.

If we've repressed any parts of ourselves, keeping them in shadow, we can tolerate them in a partner for only a short while. Then we seek to "kill off" these traits, which we recognize in the partner but not in ourselves. All too often, the relationship is the first victim.

You'll recall how I loved Mike's calmness and serenity. During our power struggle, I asked him things like, "Are you alive in there? Don't you ever feel anything?" At the start, he loved my passion, but soon he complained, "You're too emotional." He'd retreat to another room and I'd follow, demanding that we work things out. He was afraid of my insistence, and I was afraid of his walking away—fear of abandonment. As many others do, I assumed that by unleashing a verbal hailstorm I could coerce Mike into communicating. Instead, he'd become a turtle and withdraw into his shell.

In most relationships, one partner plays the turtle and the other the hailstorm. One pulls inward, and the other explodes—verbally and emotionally. (And depending on the issue, quite often the two partners can switch roles.) Hailstorms can seem scarier because they're loud and energetic. But to a hailstorm, a turtle's retreat can be just as scary—making the hailstorm feel abandoned and threatened. (Harville Hendrix created this metaphor. I use it at workshops, where it usually helps people lighten up about this common power struggle.)

Many people feel that conflict is a relationship's kiss of death. Few of us—gay men especially—realize that this dynamic is healthy. What's *not* healthy is how most people deal with it.

Yes, getting through the power struggle is very difficult. But it's the entry point to real love. It may seem easier to break off the relationship, to have an affair, or to engage in addictive behavior, rather than face your deepest conflicts and fears. The good news is that the power struggles you face with your partner actually suggest that you're with the right person for your maximum growth. You have met someone who will challenge you to make necessary changes in yourself—which can only benefit the two of you. It's an opportunity to develop closeness and intimacy while still maintaining your individuality.

Conflict is growth trying to happen. Conflict enables you to differentiate yourself from your partner, to establish boundaries, and eventually to flourish as a couple. For us gays and lesbians, who've spent our entire lives trying to conform and disown who we really are, keeping that sense of self in a relationship is even more important.

Differences can be threatening to any couple, but particularly to gay partners. Because society judges gay men as "different," we assume that differences are not OK. This in turn makes gay men wary of having to conform to anyone else's standards. But after all, isn't this what we want from our families, and from society as a whole? To be who we are, to let everyone else be who they are, and to allow the differences just to be?

Again, I am not talking about differences that are abusive. If you are in a relationship with someone who will not take responsibility or be accountable for their own behavior and instead blame you for most or all of the problems, that is about disrespect and lack of integrity on their part, not differences.

Each year in the fall, with the holidays approaching, I ask gay couples about their plans. They often speak about going home to their separate families, without each other. I always tell clients that they hired me to be controversial and challenging, so I question and challenge this—not to make them uncomfortable, but to shake things up. I want to explore whether this holiday pattern represents any internalized homophobia (it usually does). Often, I ask the couple whether they can imagine their parents going to holiday functions without each other. We all usually laugh that they might *want* to do it, but don't!

Most heterosexual couples take turns going every other year to the other family (or to both on the same day), and they go together. To gay couples, I point out that not doing so sends a message to their families and to themselves that they aren't united, or that the relationship isn't as real as the marriages of their heterosexual siblings and family members. This only weakens their relationship.

At these moments, ask yourself: Is your commitment to your partner or your family? The "family" option drains intimacy from your relationship. Straight boys and girls commit to partners their parents don't approve of, so why should we be any different? But committing to a partner brings on the power struggle!

A family's failure to recognize their gay loved one's partnership as a valid relationship manifests in many ways. A gay son's family often views him as "single," even if he's partnered. Typically, he doesn't have children, hasn't had a wedding ceremony, and may not even verbalize that his relationship is a partnership of love. Often, a gay partner sees his relationship as inferior to those of his married siblings. It's up to you to present yourself and your partner as a family unit.

Kenny and Brad had been together two years when they came to see me. Kenny was completely out to his family, but Brad wasn't out to his. They were having problems because the year before he met Kenny, Brad ended a five-year relationship. At gatherings, Brad's family—not realizing the facts—constantly asked about Charlie, who to them was just a friend of Brad's who had come to all the past family functions. Kenny became angry at having to listen to Brad's family go on and on about how much they liked Charlie.

A straight man usually introduces the woman he's dating as his girlfriend. If they break up, he tells his family about it and introduces his next companion as his girlfriend too. It's clear she's the new woman in his life—and families are usually tactful enough not to ask about his old flame in front of the new one! As a result of this conflict, Brad and Kenny's lines of communication had broken down, which diminished their feelings of safety and mutual trust.

After the three of us worked together for several months, their ability to communicate improved. Their connections to each other—and their sense of safety and trust—returned. But Kenny continued to express frustration about Brad's reluctance to tell his family that he was gay, that Kenny was his partner, and that they were a family unit.

Yes, "family" is definitely the word to use. (I often hear straight couples without children referring to themselves as families.) In the gay community, we couples call ourselves "family" to help people—and ourselves—recognize that there are all kinds of valid families. And a gay couple is one of them.

However, with the Christmas and Hanukkah holidays approaching, I asked my usual question: "What are you going to do?" They replied that each would still visit his own family on his own. They also disclosed that neither family gave gifts to the other man's partner. Worse still, Brad's family continued to purchase gifts for Charlie every Christmas.

Ultimately, Brad decided it was time to come out to his parents. This was very difficult for him on various levels and for various reasons. But he knew that his relationship would only get stronger if he reinforced the idea that he'd started his own family.

I haven't worked with Brad and Kenny for a number of years, but recently I received an invitation to their commitment ceremony—to which they invited their friends and both their families. They had come a long way!

Introducing your partner as a "friend" indicates that he's not special enough for you to tell the truth. And postponing this kind of challenge means it will only come back in a more powerful form.

At the talks I give to gays and lesbians, I strongly stress the importance of making partnerships clear to hosts who send invitations. It's inappropriate to say "and guest," or to use two separate invitations when inviting a couple. But it's up to you to inform whoever sends the invitations that you *are* part of a couple. It's not fair to assume they should know, and many people are simply unsure how to handle the situation. (Except for the very supportive columnist Judith Martin, who writes as "Miss Manners," there is no etiquette guru who instructs straight people on how to treat gay couples with the same grace and tact that straight couples routinely enjoy.)

If you're faced with such a dilemma, my advice is to call the sender and ask simply, "Please send the invitation to both of us."

When I was first partnered, I did exactly that. I sent out holiday cards from Mike and me—that is, from both of us. If one of my relatives sent me an invitation, I called to let them know that I was partnered, and that I'd like to bring Mike to the event. Next time, could they please invite us both? Some of my relatives were not OK with this, which was tough.

I knew up front that I was taking a risk. But simply knowing you're taking that risk makes the risk less risky! If Mike wasn't invited to an event, I wouldn't go either. That sent a strong message to my relatives—and to Mike—that we were now a family of our own. I wouldn't accept less respect than they would show a heterosexual couple.

Maya Kollman, a therapist for 25 years, trained me to become a Certified Imago Relationship Therapist. In her article "Helping Couples Get the Love They Want," she writes, "The Imago process is particularly useful for our community because same-sex couples, who experience all the typical ups and downs of opposite-sex couples, are expected to cope with these challenges without the same ample support systems straights have. Often they feel isolated, adrift on a desert island. Teaching them the Imago model is like offering these castaways the tools they need to build a paradise of connection."[2]

I love that notion! With so many negative influences bearing down on our relationships, we must find the support we need wherever we can. Both personally and professionally, I am deeply grateful for the Imago's optimistic, people-oriented model—one of the best therapeutic interventions to help our relationships evolve into mature love.

References

1. Harville Hendrix, *Getting the Love You Want: A Guide for Couples*. New York: Henry Holt and Company (1988).

2. Maya Kollman, "Helping Couples Get the Love They Want," *In the Family* magazine, April 1997.

Chapter 10
Commit to a Partner

I WISH YOU STRAIGHT PEOPLE WOULD STOP TRYING TO
PREVENT US FROM MARRYING EACH OTHER. IF YOU LET US
MARRY EACH OTHER, THEN WE WILL STOP MARRYING YOU!
—gay comedian Jason Stuart

When I heard that joke, my mind flashed to all my gay clients who have been heterosexually married. The heterosexually married gay man is in a bind. If you think about it, he's in a mixed marriage: He's gay, and she's straight. Thus the intensity of the couple's intimacy is limited. The connection between the two pales in comparison to the fulfillment he could have with another man (and she could have with a man who's thoroughly heterosexual).

Yet most formerly married gay men admit that in some ways, they're glad they married. They enjoyed all that went with it—their weddings, the birth of their children, family support, and a stable, secure home life. As married heterosexuals, they didn't have to worry about prejudice when their spouses telephoned at work, came to holiday parties, or gave them photographs to display on their desks. Typically, married clients worry that such satisfactions can't be re-created in gay culture.

As gay men, it's possible to have all that—though it involves a bit more work for us than for our heterosexual counterparts. Everyone needs to understand that the more he commits to a partner, the harder their relationship becomes. But as you saw in the last chapter, the difficult parts can be positive and healthy. You just need to know how best to navigate through them.

Straight or gay, we all yearn to be in lasting love relationships. Gays are regularly assaulted with charges that we're promiscuous and that all we want is anonymous sex. Then, when we push for monogamous relationships to be not just honored but legalized, we're told we can't have them! We're the only minority that mainstream society criticizes for longing to be in committed relationships with others of our own culture.

Many clients who were once heterosexually married say that issues arising in their gay relationships are similar to ones they grappled with during their marriages to women. But now the issues are more intense. Being with someone of the same gender provides gay men with a better Imago match. The romance is more exhilarating—and the power struggle more acute. But they usually report that the exchange is well worth the hassle, because they know they're with the right person.

Greg, a tall, handsome home builder, knew he was gay, but had hoped he would change. Over the years various therapists told him his same-sex attraction was a "phase." He believed them and, hoping that they were right, married a woman whom he deeply loved. During their years together they tried to have children but couldn't. Though he was faithful to his wife, he fantasized about men throughout their relationship. Now, at age 36, he'd fallen in love with a man. This challenge to their marriage had put distance between him and his wife, but Greg felt comfortable with the situation and made no attempts to get closer to her. Nor did she try to bridge the chasm between them.

But his wife had a very close relationship with their dog. Greg knew it was odd to feel jealous of an animal; he wanted the attention his wife was giving their dog but not him. When she tried to engage him in an attempt to find out what was wrong, Greg didn't want to talk. He didn't think the effort was worth it.

Over time, their sexual relationship came to a halt, and neither one attempted to mend this breach. Greg recognized there were problems in this marriage, but something stopped him from doing anything to resolve them. He believed his homosexuality was strictly sexual and that he could manage by keeping it to himself. Only after he met and fell in love with Eric, a plumbing contractor who was also married with a young son, did Greg realize that his homosexuality was emotional as well as sexual.

He and Eric met at a new home that Greg was constructing, and they immediately hit it off. The two started to spend time together, working out, golfing, going to movies, and sharing drinks. They convinced themselves that they were just friends. Eventually Greg began to compare what he had with Eric to his relationship with his wife. In time, he reconciled that he was in fact gay, divorced his wife, and entered a relationship with Eric.

The romantic love between them, Greg said, was something he'd never experienced before, and their sex was passionate. But when their romantic love stage ended, the inevitable power struggle surfaced. Distance developed between them. As with his ex-wife and their dog, Greg began to resent Eric's attention to his son's needs. This time, however, Greg tried to talk to Eric about his jealousy. Discussion always led to an argument, which left both men feeling insecure and even more distant. Their sex life understandably diminished. Greg found himself facing a familiar problem even in a dramatically different relationship.

The distance between him and his ex-wife had caused him no pain at all. But the pain he felt in his relationship with Eric was excruciating. He kept trying to get Eric to talk. But they weren't able to communicate, and their estrangement only grew worse. Eric felt pain too. Neither wanted the relationship to end. Greg suggested that they both enter couples therapy.

Heterosexually married gay men and gay men who've enjoyed long-term friendships with women have an advantage. If one or both partners have emerged from a heterosexual marriage, they tend to be more engaged in their current relationship. They're simply more compassionate, adaptable, and accommodating.

I think these skills are taught (if not demanded!) by the women in their lives. Gay men who don't have this experience with straight women must learn these traits and techniques on their own.

Of the 22 participants at one of my gay men's weekend workshops, 18 were still in heterosexual marriages, were just ending them, or had ended them some time ago. Compared to other workshop participants, they were much more punctual. They showed more consideration for one another and for the workshop staff. They were mindful of the time they spent talking and sharing and, overall, showed a better understanding of the work involved.

When a gay client doesn't think gay men can commit deeply, I throw some facts his way. For 30 years, John Gottman, a well-known psychologist, has worked with heterosexual couples and, in the last decade, with gay and lesbian couples too. His work is research-based, using observable, quantitative measurements. He brought couples to a "love lab"—essentially, a pleasant bed-and-breakfast. Each couple interacted with their partner while hooked up to various machines that monitored their heart rates and perspiration levels.

Gottman's findings are an important, welcome addition to the chronicle of same-gender relationships. In his work with Robert Levenson, Gottman showed that gay and lesbian couples have some advantages over their heterosexual counterparts.[1] To determine why relationships succeed or fail, Gottman and Levenson assessed 21 gay and 21 lesbian couples over 12 years—based on direct observations of their expressions and tones of voice, self-reports, interviews, and videotaped interaction. They compared these to a "control" group of 42 straight couples—a total of 84 couples, each together at least two years.

Gay couples were comparable to heterosexual couples in the quality of their relationships; they report the same happiness and satisfaction. Interestingly, gay couples weren't as prone to jealousy. If a straight guy says, "That woman's really stacked," his wife will give him a hard time. If a woman comments on another man's nice "package" or "six-pack abs," the man in her life may feel hurt and may or may not make a fuss. By contrast, two gay men can admire another man and comment on how attractive he is, but neither takes it personally or feels threatened.

Among heterosexual couples I've treated, women often feel that by commenting on another woman's good looks, their husbands literally cheat on them. Gay and lesbian couples may show some reactivity to such remarks, but usually much less.

Same-gender couples, Gottman and Levenson found, were much better at talking openly and honestly about their sex lives. In an article by Mubarak Dahir in the *Windy City Times,* Gottman remarked, "When we videotape a heterosexual couple talking about lovemaking, you have no idea what they are talking about."[2] We're of the same gender, with the same orgasmic reactions, timing, and sensations. Heterosexual couples have less understanding of each other and function differently.

Gottman and Levenson provide another eye-opener. Over their 12-year study, only 20% of the gay and lesbian couples broke up, compared to 38% of heterosexual couples. At the study's end, almost twice as many straight couples were no longer together. In the face of adversity, gay and lesbian couples were much more optimistic. When addressing conflicts between them, they used more humor and affection.

Before leaving my office at the end of a session, lesbian couples generally hug each other. I've learned from that and encourage gay male couples to do the same. At the very least, one will crack a joke and both will laugh—which can be just as effective. Only rarely have I been able to get heterosexual couples to do this after a session.

Gottman and Levenson also found that gay and lesbian couples take things less personally. I've found this more common with gay male couples. Gay men—again, because we're conditioned to behave like all other men—can shrug off an argument and not take it too much to heart. But I've spent countless hours of therapy trying to help lesbian couples not take things so very personally. On the other hand, gay males too often tend to shrug off arguments, and I must help them see things a little more personally to be sure that they'll work through important issues.

Ted and David would cruise a popular gay resort looking for men who were interested in three-ways. David wasn't happy with this, but

Ted insisted they go. Eventually, David stopped trying to get Ted to see his point of view and just went along. I had to emphasize that cruising for three-ways wasn't the problem—the problem was that David wasn't a consenting partner. He needed help to confront Ted's lack of interest in his personal feelings. Without my intervention, this behavior would have continued, with David and their relationship both suffering.

Luke and Tony let their dog sleep in their bed with them at night. It was actually Tony's idea. Both of them found it cute at first, but Luke began to feel uncomfortable. He'd want to cuddle or initiate sexual contact, only to find Tony cuddling with the dog. To have sex at night, they'd put the dog in another room, but he would whine and want to come in.

Luke tried to talk to Tony about this, but to no avail. Ultimately, he totally subordinated his emotional needs and let the issue drop. His job required a lot of travel away from home, so he rationalized that sharing their bed with the dog was the "least he could do for Tony," thereby minimizing the problem this sleeping arrangement caused their relationship. Again, I urged Luke to talk to Tony about his feelings and not to let the situation continue.

Gottman and Levenson observed that "In a fight, lesbians show more anger, humor, excitement, and interest than conflicting gay men. This suggests that lesbians are more emotionally expressive—positively and negatively—than gay men. This may result from having two women in a relationship. Both have been raised in a society where expressiveness is more acceptable for women...." Their research revealed that gay male couples "aren't as adept in repairing relationships after negativity. Gay men may need extra help to offset the impact of negative emotions that inevitably come along when couples fight."[3]

In my practice I've also noted that male couples do tend to have difficulty getting over negativity after an argument. In relationships, the female usually pushes to talk directly and express feelings. Without her energy, these factors must be consciously brought into a gay male relationship. As a therapist, I often feel like the woman, pushing gay men to appropriate these techniques into their relationships.

Every couple I see has both male and female energy—even gay male couples. Female and male energies are more about what Western society calls feminine or masculine. For example, we think of women as homemakers and men as breadwinners. But plenty of men—straight and gay alike—prefer being homemakers. In our society, we call that feminine energy. But even if the male is a carrier of female energy, he doesn't necessarily have the skills that women have been socialized to possess.

There are usually more lesbians in my workshops for gay and lesbian couples. I take that to indicate that women are socialized to value relationships more. During check-in at one workshop, a lesbian couple said they were breaking up and had come to salvage their friendship. They reported that they'd spent 25 years together and wanted to leave with integrity, maintaining the strong connection they'd had before—only now in a different way. I was impressed that they were so mature and respectful of their past relationship.

Again, there's nothing inherently gay or lesbian about this. It's strictly a male-female distinction. Women are encouraged to be in touch with their emotions, value close relations, and be considerate of the other people in their lives. Men are raised to be competitive, goal-oriented, sexually aggressive breadwinners who keep their emotions inside. As a result, many gay males overwork, focus on outer tasks rather than inner ones, have sex outside of their relationships, and seldom express emotions to their partners (or to themselves or anyone else, for that matter!).

I've also noticed that most gay men are very capable of engaging in dialogue, being compassionate, and bonding emotionally to others. We're often much more in touch with our emotions than straight men, but in our adult love relationships it's a whole different story. We haven't been encouraged to bond deeply with other men—in fact, just the opposite. Because of homophobia, we're taught from an early age not to hug or kiss other boys, express emotion to them, or talk to guys about our inner lives. We bring all this baggage, along with our family upbringing, into any love relationship.

Harville Hendrix addresses the question of "exits": behaviors that individuals use to remove themselves from relationships—emotionally and/or physically. In *Getting the Love You Want*, he writes, "An exit is acting out one's feelings rather than putting them into language."[4]

If you can't express anger toward someone, you'll inevitably act out the emotion in that person's absence. (The classic example is the man who, after his boss chews him out at work, comes home and kicks his dog.) Or else you'll act it out sideways, through passive-aggressive behavior. If you find yourself doing this, it doesn't mean that you're a bad person, you're just scared and hesitant. Exits are simply ways of avoiding intimacy.

Most affairs are merely the symptom of an unhealthy relationship. Both parties are involved, inasmuch as neither is addressing the real issues in the partnership. One or both partners may be engaging in outside activity (in this case, an affair) to express resentment and frustration—in a nonproductive way, obviously. An affair is always an impediment to one's relationship, particularly if it's secretive. No steady relationship in the power struggle can compete with an affair, which will always make the relationship look less exciting. An affair is romantic love, but with a weak, tenuous commitment, fueled mostly by PEA.

Meanwhile, the relationship is usually working through the power struggle stage. Understandably, partners will put more energy into an affair, which feels good, rather than into a power struggle, which feels bad.

Exits are a universal phenomenon. We all employ them—usually unconsciously. Like affairs, they arise most often when two people move from romantic love to the power struggle and come up against intimacy issues within the relationship. Exits reduce the power struggle's intensity and pain, basically by watering down the dependency in the relationship.

There are plenty of ways to get on an exit ramp. In the least extreme instances, they take the form of shopping, working out, devoting time to pets or relatives' kids, or pursuing a new hobby. What's wrong with these normal behaviors? Not the activities themselves, but the excessiveness that induces you to spend time away from your partner.

I often treat gay couples where one partner is overinvolved in community service or work, or the other dotes on a pet, spends more time with his children than his partner, or gardens every daylight hour on the weekend.

How can you distinguish reasonable activity from an exit? Either you must admit to yourself that you're using these activities to escape, or your partner must tell you. If I'm doing too many weekend workshops, my partner Mike taps me gently on the shoulder and says, "Another weekend away from me?" In the past, I used to tell him "The gay community needs this. I have to do it!" or "This is my job." Both statements are true, but I had no idea how my being away so often was affecting us.

The point that Mike was making—which I finally got—wasn't that I needed to stop doing weekend workshops, but that I needed not to do them so frequently. Mike encouraged me to spend more time with him—which I needed and wanted to do. If he hadn't pointed this out, I wouldn't have realized how I was exiting our relationship.

Other exit strategies coincide with common troublemaking behaviors. For example, if a man constantly threatens to leave his partner, or tells himself he can always get out of the relationship—in short, if he thinks of breaking up before he gives the relationship a full chance—he unconsciously builds his partnership to resemble a mild form of divorce.

The exit impulse can also take the form of basic aggression, domestic violence, or emotional and verbal abuse. "Accidental" carelessness—a form of passive aggression—also fits here. We see this behavior in the man who forgets his partner's birthday or, worse, who cheats on him and comes home to have unprotected sex. Obviously, this puts the unsuspecting partner at great risk for various sexually transmitted diseases (STDs), including HIV. This can be lethal—not only to the relationship.

Less severe but still destructive are poor self-care (such as not getting regular medical checkups and not maintaining one's physical body through exercise) and passive indifference to emotional problems such as depression or anxiety. Untreated addictions also serve as effective exits. Is a man more committed to alcohol, drugs, sex, gambling, or food than to his partner? Again, addiction diminishes the intimacy that any relationship demands.

Some clients complain that their relationships literally drive them crazy. When I think of insanity, I prefer the concept used in 12 Step groups: engaging in the same behaviors—doing the same thing over and over—and expecting different results. (I think cheating on one's partner while not engaging in safe sex is also a form of insanity. Even if putting him at risk isn't the exiting partner's intent, denying that possibility is insane.) I am not talking about psychotic insanity here, where one hallucinates, is delusional, or loses touch with reality. Neurotic insanity is being in touch with reality but still engaging in behaviors you know you shouldn't.

If you find yourself involved in one or more of these exits, it's very important that you not begin to think of yourself as a bad person. These behaviors simply indicate trouble in your relationship or within yourself. You (with or without your partner, as a couple) need professional help.

Harville Hendrix talks about the "no exit decision." To commit more fully to your relationship, you must begin a discussion about closing off your exits. We recognize that not all exits can be closed that easily! So a more appropriate expectation is a "no exit discussion." For instance, if your partner's drinking too much or doing drugs, you and he can begin to talk about the effects of his behavior on your relationship. Then solutions, healing, and re-entry into intimacy can begin as energy starts moving away from whatever exits he's engaged in.

Closing exits is a process, not an event. It can take a while to close an exit—usually the exit's there for a reason, to meet a need or avoid a hurt. Whatever the reason, you should address it, bring it to consciousness, and examine how it's impacting you and your partner. Just discussing it with him brings energy back into your relationship.

Many people enter partnerships with their exits already up and running. Many addictions and mood disorders such as depression or anxiety lie dormant prior to a relationship. During the relationship they may surface or worsen in response to the demand for intimacy. This is not the result of a bad relationship but rather an opportunity to look at why we engage in intimacy-avoidance behaviors and to look at what it means to have a deep level of intimacy in our lives.

Exits are mostly the result of the conflict between your desire to be with a partner and your fear of being in a relationship. The more you commit, the more childhood feelings, memories, and experiences tend to surface, because you have increased your dependency onto your partner. For many of us, saying "I want intimacy" or "I want a relationship" is frightening. The more abusive and traumatic your childhood, the greater your fear of committing yourself. Going back there is really scary!

Because gay boys were taught to avoid other gays early on, pursuing another man goes directly against that imprint. We manage the problem in different ways. Creating exits in our relationships lets us tolerate the closeness that troubles us. Our conscious "adult" side says, "Nothing to be afraid of. I'm in the relationship of my dreams!" But our unconscious, emotional side says, "This is childhood all over again. I feel endangered!"

John was confused. Was his relationship in trouble? Or was his own "baggage"—his sexual addiction—the source of the problem? John, who owned a tax-preparation franchise, had been with Kyle for almost six years. He admitted to never feeling the romantic love that other men seemed to feel for their partners. He had talked to friends, seen movies, and read books about the initial honeymoon period—and that simply didn't correspond to the start of his relationship with Kyle. But John hadn't found this a problem because he was a sex addict at the time! He'd partnered with a man who wanted strict monogamy and wasn't as sexual as he was.

This apparent mismatch is very common. Many sex addicts unconsciously or consciously choose partners with conservative religious and/or moral convictions, a lower libido, or more rigid ideas of what lovemaking should be. It's a way for the sex addict to unconsciously manage his addiction. (The more repressed partner may well be unconsciously titillated by the addict's wider sexual experiences, which let him enjoy—albeit vicariously—escapades that he'd never allow himself in real life.)

John entered his relationship with a problem. On some level, he sought his partner's help in managing it. At the start of their relationship, John could stop his sexual acting-out. He wanted to be more like Kyle—earnestly monogamous and clear about what healthy sex should be. But after two years John returned to the bars, with friends or alone, to pick up men for anonymous hookups.

Unable to stop, he became guilt-stricken. He felt the loss of control that comes from sexual addiction. In addition, he started cruising other men and flirting with them in front of his partner. Kyle claimed he didn't mind that John enjoyed the attention, but he didn't appreciate the actual flirting and cruising.

Kyle tolerated John's behavior without accepting it. John continued to flirt and cruise, despite Kyle's objections and hurt feelings. Neither talked about the issue, because whenever they'd tried the discussion always ended in an argument. If they did mention the subject, it was in passive-aggressive, oblique, noncommunicative ways.

Clearly, John's relationship with Kyle hadn't created his sexual addiction, though it soon became a stumbling block for them both. During therapy, we discovered that at the age of 9 John had been sexually abused by a male baby-sitter. He recalled being tied down while the sitter fondled and orally raped him. The young man warned John that if he told, the sitter would kill his dog. This helped us see why he now engaged in sexual acting-out and also why John had a hard time hearing his partner's concerns. A major issue in his relationship—and ultimately, in his therapy—was that he didn't like being told what to do. To his ears, Kyle's bids for him to stop cruising sounded more like an order rather than the request of a hurt partner who wanted deeper intimacy. In essence, John was feeling "tied down."

Once John began to deal with his sexual abuse, he was able to work on his relationship. Both he and Kyle came to my couple's workshop and went to couples therapy with another therapist. (Kyle wasn't comfortable coming to see me because I had seen John individually for a long time.) Now they were able to close that particular exit.

Once he discovered how his sexual acting-out related to childhood abuse, John was able to work more successfully on stopping it. For his part, Kyle learned to overcome his impulse to keep silent about important things that caused him problems and frustration. Together they salvaged their relationship and moved into a deeper commitment.

While John and Kyle did not experience romantic love initially, that did not mean they were in the wrong relationship. Some do not aspire to romantic love (also referred to as "limerence"); they see it as unproductive and distracting.

Yes, commitment is difficult! The more we commit, the deeper the power struggle, which raises more conflict. If problems remain unresolved, our relationship no longer feels emotionally safe. Communication breaks down. Distrust sets in. This becomes the natural state of dysfunctional relationships. This is where couples usually are when they come to me.

Imago Relationship Therapy has a wonderful communication exercise that I use with most every couple—actually, it's the foundation to all Imago techniques. This "Intentional Couples Dialogue" has three parts: mirroring, validation, and empathy. It offers couples ways to communicate through dialogue, not monologue.

When our partner tries to convey a message, most often we're waiting our turn—not truly listening. We sit in our own reactivity, not truly hearing our partners' voice. This is monological communication.

By contrast, dialogue involves mirroring. One partner sends information, on one topic, in short declarative sentences starting with "I," until he's entirely finished. The receiver doesn't interpret, diminish, or magnify the message, but simply reflects what's said until the sender says, "There's no more."

Deceptively simple! But therapists do it all the time. You'd learn these basic reflective listening skills in an emergency crisis center. Carl Rogers, a well known psychologist, found people felt more connected and understood when therapists used these reflective listening techniques. It was brilliant for him to suggest that partners use it with one another.

What did your partner say? "I'm upset that you don't appreciate it when I clean up." As the receiver, you say, "You don't feel I appreciate your cleaning up the house. And you're upset?" Then you add, "Did I get it? Is there more?"

This doesn't stop until the sender feels heard and understood.

Asking, "Did I get it?" sends the message that you're really trying to understand what your partner's saying. "Is there more?" tells him that your ears are open and you do want to hear.

The second part of intentional dialogue is validation. After your partner finishes speaking, you validate what you heard, from his point of view. For most people, this is difficult. You respond, "What you're saying makes sense. I can see why you'd think this way." This isn't necessarily agreement—you simply validate your partner's point of view. You look through his eyes to affirm the way he views the world. Yours isn't the only way to view conflicts in your relationship!

Because we gays and lesbians have been told over and over that what we think and feel is wrong, validating can be hard. Saying to someone "That makes sense" can feel like a stretch, especially when you don't agree. In our society, we assume that what makes one person right makes another wrong.

The last part of the technique is empathy. Imagine what your partner might be feeling, given what he's said. You validate not just his words but his feelings. We men aren't taught to do this as well as women, so as a therapist, I spend lots of time helping men learn to be empathic with one another. After the sender is finished and the receiver has mirrored, validated, and empathized, the couple switches roles. Sender becomes receiver and receiver becomes sender. Still on the same topic, so as not to stack up issues, allowing both partners' realities to exist on the one topic.

Mike and I first learned couples dialogue at a weekend workshop that I had to attend to become an Imago therapist. I recall thinking, If Mike and I are in such bad shape that we have to talk like this for the rest of our lives, then it's not worth it! It felt tedious and mechanical. And it is! But after practicing it for a while, we realized that it helped us to hear each other more accurately and deeply. Now we use it only if we're too reactive. It's saved us from a lot of fights that before would have left both of us with hurt feelings.

If you want to speak to your partner, make an appointment. Sounds trite, but it works. The partner who has a frustration tells the other what's going on. "Is this is a good time to discuss it?" If the other partner says no, the two negotiate for a better time. We recommend that couples not wait more than 24 hours.

Once couples move through the power struggle stage, then they can commit even more deeply. Following are some ways to accomplish this.

What do you call your man? "Lover" was most commonly used until the 1990s. During the 1990s, we've seen a shift from "lover" to "partner." In her book *Permanent Partners,* Betty Berzon attributes this shift to the legalization of live-together relationships. Gays and lesbians began to realize the need to protect themselves and their partners legally, but the word "lover" was inappropriate in legal documents.[5] Thus "partner" became more widely used.

As a gay man, I wear a wedding ring and expect my partner to be invited to all events I'm invited to. And I enjoy talking about Mike to others. Society may tell me that I'm pushing my relationship in people's faces when all I've ever wanted are the very same rights, privileges, and recognition that my sister and her spouse enjoy. Legally married, she wears her wedding band, talks openly about her husband, and brings him to all special events and family gatherings. No one would think of saying to her, "Honey, we don't want to hear about your sex life. So take off that wedding band. Don't talk about your husband.

And don't expect to bring him around, because we don't want to see him. You're just shoving your sexuality down our throats."

I want to publicly celebrate my love for Mike. And I want to share in Mike's insurance benefits. If he dies before I do, I won't receive any of his Social Security benefits, as a legal widow would. I want to help make decisions should Mike fall ill or be injured. But as a "single" person, not legally bound to him, I have none of these rights. A hospital could deny me entry to his room because I'm not legally part of his family. He and I have taken care of this in our wills and have legal power of attorney for each other, so I could go to court to prove our agreement—but what a hassle! Worries like this cause stress in a relationship.

Both in and outside my practice, I'm often shocked to meet gay couples who've been together for a number of years, who share a home and expenses, yet still refer to themselves as "boyfriends." To me, a boyfriend is someone you date. Using words like "friend" or "boyfriend" minimizes the level of your commitment and throws up a barrier to deeper levels of intimacy.

Whether you're straight or gay, it's always easier to decide not to commit more deeply. For one thing, being noncommittal allows you a handy, guilt-free exit: "Well, if this doesn't work out, I can always leave. This relationship isn't like a real marriage, so I don't have to abide by any rules." Marriage helps couples achieve a psychological intimacy they might not otherwise experience. First of all, merely considering marriage promotes a deeper commitment between the two partners. Deciding to go for it prompts all kinds of new hopes, questions, and insecurities.

By committing more fully to a male partner and thereby becoming more visible and "out," you'll face hurdles you'd never encounter if you were straight. Heterosexual brides and their fiancés are usually overwhelmed by the demands of their respective families. If anyone asked them, "Does your wedding have a political agenda?" they'd be surprised at such a ridiculous question. For gays and lesbians, however, just the idea of having a wedding is politically loaded. I've heard many gay men use this as the reason not to have a ceremony. I believe that rationale is often just another exit—a way of avoiding a deeper commitment to oneself and to one's partner.

Marriage isn't for everyone, but Gottman's research shows that heterosexual couples who simply live together (or "cohabitate") are more likely to break up than couples who commit more deeply. Again, our deepest healing as individuals—and especially as gay men—is achieved in a committed adult love relationship.

At the time I write this, we gay folk are not afforded legal marriage anywhere in the United States. In the Netherlands, gay marriage is allowed—but that status is not honored anywhere else in the world. Vermont grants "civil unions," but it is the only state that recognizes the legality of such partnerships. Imagine the outrage if heterosexuals married and traveled to another state or country, only to find their marriage annulled as soon as they crossed the border!

Every marriage has two parts: the ceremonial and the legal. Since we're denied the legal part, we can still benefit from the ceremonial part, which can be either secular or religious. Based on his and Levenson's research with gay and lesbian couples, Gottman affirms that we can deepen our commitments without being legally married.

When I say "marriage," I hasten to add that I don't care what you call your ceremony. Use whatever works for you. For the sake of this discussion, I'll use "marriage," since that's what works for me. The idea is to have a ceremony with the elements and overtones of a wedding.

Planning a marriage will recall your earlier romantic times, but it will also deepen your power struggle because you're tightening the space between the two of you! The experience will stir events from childhood, when you first encountered this type of relational closeness. The type of family you grew up in will determine how you react to the new dynamics in your current relationship.

When Larry and Curt first met they fell madly in love—romantic love, that is. Larry adored Curt's assertiveness and found him to be a very passionate man. Curt loved Larry's independence. They enjoyed a wonderful year of togetherness. When they agreed to live together, they decided to go all the way and get married. As they moved forward with their wedding plans, Larry began to see Curt's assertiveness as domineering. And to Curt, Larry's independence began to feel like lack of interest.

During therapy with me, they discovered something that surprised them both. Larry had been raised by a dominant, authoritarian father who was extremely rule-oriented and who demanded things go his way. Suddenly Larry began to perceive these same traits in Curt. Yes, Curt was passionate about things he wanted for the wedding, but he wasn't being domineering. Yet Larry took it that way—clearly a projection we needed to work through in therapy.

Curt was raised by an uninvolved mother who neglected him through most of his childhood. He was better at planning and had more ideas for the wedding; therefore Larry tended to defer to him. But instead of seeing Larry's easygoing cooperation for what it was, Curt felt that he was being ignored and left to his own devices. He too was regressing to childhood. As you'll recall from Chapter 9, this kind of power struggle is supposed to happen and is a positive indicator of a healthy relationship. But while it's happening, it's not much fun.

Mike and I ran into similar challenges in planning our wedding. First, what were we going to call our upcoming celebration? Some gays and lesbians call it a commitment ceremony, others call it a union. We were a couple of traditional guys; for us, the words "wedding" and "marriage" seemed most apt.

Since both of us are men, we knew nothing about planning a wedding. Women (especially the mother of the bride) tend to be the driving force behind weddings. They talk to their girlfriends, sisters, and mothers and support one another in the planning. Magazines typically focus on the bride, as does the language of marriage: bridal showers, bridal party, bridal gown. We resolved that problem by hiring a party planner to take care of all the details. Having a third party involved also reduced the amount of conflict between us and our families in handling the wedding plans. And gratefully, it worked!

Next, we had to decide where to hold the wedding. Thankfully,

Reform Judaism recognizes gay marriages, and I am a Reform Jew. Our wonderful rabbi agreed to perform the ceremony.

We considered ourselves engaged and decided to publicly declare our engagement in print, as other couples do. So we sent our picture and announcement to a local newspaper, who returned them with the reply, "We are not ready for this right now."

Though this hurt us deeply, Mike and I didn't allow this setback to stop us. Our next step was to select a gay-friendly photographer, videographer, florist, and band. Our party planner assumed the risk of facing homophobia in his search. And sure enough, he did. I told him to assure prospective candidates that ours would be a traditional, conservative wedding where nothing "unusual" would occur.

Because many people equate "gay" with sex, their minds focus only on that aspect of our lives. Our planner reported he'd had the most problems with musicians who were concerned about witnessing the "emotion between two men." We realized this isn't really a gay issue: The society we live in simply doesn't honor or support affection between men in general. Even with limited choices, our planner helped us find an excellent band.

Instead of tossing the bouquet and garter belt (neither of which figured into our plans), we decided to throw Bert and Ernie from Sesame Street. A few years before our wedding some organizations had "outed" them as a gay couple. ("They take baths together and sleep in the same bed together; this is modeling homosexuality.") We honored Bert and Ernie as a fine "gay couple" and asked our florist to create table settings using small Bert and Ernie puppets and a Tinky Winky doll, all tied together in a bow with a tag honoring them as "A Perfect Family."

Registering for our gifts required a few changes, as did the marriage contract. We laughed when the forms asked for the names of bride and groom. Whoever filled it out made the other partner the bride. Though we did have some fun with this, it seemed sad that wedding jargon makes no room for gay couples. Someday, we hope, there'll be options for grooms and grooms, and brides and brides.

Next came the bachelor parties. Because we're both men, we had one party for us both. The wife of one straight male friend had banned him from bachelor parties, because he had gotten into trouble in the past—but she had no qualms about his attending a gay male bachelor party!

Everything else went smoothly. Mike and I were married under a traditional *chuppah,* or wedding canopy, supported by four firm poles over the *bimah,* or altar, where synagogue weddings take place. Our family and friends were all there, and we felt loved and supported. We wanted to be open about our love and commitment. We wanted a place at the table—and we took it for ourselves!

There's a great song, written by a man named Fred Small, called "Everything Possible." It used to be sung by a gay and lesbian group called the Flirtations, who are no longer together. I use it at the end of my workshops and, because I think the song applies to us all, I'm including it here in its entirety:

We have cleared off the table, the leftovers saved
Washed the dishes and put them away
I have told you a story and tucked you in tight
At the end of your knockabout day
As the moon sets its sails to carry you to sleep
Over the midnight sea
I will sing you a song no one sang to me
May it keep you good company

You can be anybody you want to be
You can love whomever you will
You can travel any country where your heart leads
And know I will love you still
You can live by yourself, you can gather friends around
You can choose one special one
And the only measure of your words and your deeds
Will be the love you leave behind when you're done

There are girls who grow up strong and bold
There are boys quiet and kind

Some race on ahead, some follow behind
Some go in their own way and time
Some women love women, some men love men
Some raise children, some never do
You can dream all the day never reaching the end
Of everything possible for you

Don't be rattled by names, by taunts, by games
But seek out spirits true
If you give your friends the best part of yourself
They will give the same back to you.

Nobody ever sang that song to me, but now I sing it to myself. And I will sing it to my nephews, Jacob and Zachary.

We all need to hear these words.

References

1. See www.gottman.com.

2. Mubarak Dahir, "A Gay Thing," in *The Windy City Times,* February 21, 2001.

3. See www.gottman.com, "What Makes Same-Sex Relationships Succeed or Fail."

4. Harville Hendrix, *Getting the Love You Want: A Guide for Couples.* New York: Henry Holt & Co. (1988).

5. Betty Berzon, *Permanent Partners: Building Gay and Lesbian Relationships That Last.* New York: Penguin Books, 1988.

Acknowledgments

This book is dedicated to Mike Cramer, my partner, with whom I've lived and learned these Ten Things, and whose love and patience sustained me throughout. You have taught me about integrity, trust, and commitment. You have taught me what family really means. You make the world safe for me.

To Jim Gerardi, who encouraged me to write the book and got me started on it; and to Alan Semonian, whose advice and friendship have been so important.

I want to express special thanks to my beloved sister Lisa Kort-Jaisinghani and her family, especially my nephews Jacob, Zachary, and Noah, whose sweet presence in my life is such a blessing.

To Barb Shumard, MSW, whose supervision and guidance allowed me to mature and grow as a therapist and to help the clients who seek my services.

To Lynn Grodzki, MSW, whose coaching and teaching lay the groundwork that made it possible for me to write this book.

I'm especially grateful to all the gay men and gay couples whose courageous work I have been privileged to witness. I have been honored to be a part of your lives and to help you grow into the fine gay men who now surround me in the gay community. I have learned a great deal from you. Thank you.

Finally, I want to acknowledge my mother-in-law, Lee Cramer, who is not here to read my completed work and who was one of my biggest champions when I decided to write this book.